CONTINUITIES

Essays and Ideas in American Literature

Marvin Fisher

UNIVERSITY
PRESS OF
AMERICA

LANHAM • NEW YORK • LONDON

Copyright © 1986 by

University Press of America,® Inc.

4720 Boston Way
Lanham, MD 20706

3 Henrietta Street
London WC2E 8LU England

Library of Congress Cataloging in Publication Data

Fisher, Marvin, 1927-
    Continuities : essays and ideas in American
literature.

    Most essays previously published.
    Bibliography: p.
    Contents: The pattern of conservatism in Johnson's
Rasselas and Hawthorne's tales—"Bartleby,"
Melville's circumscribed scrivener — "Benito Cereno" —
[etc.]
    1. American literature—History and criticism—
Addresses, essays, lectures.   2. American literature—
19th century—History and criticism—Addresses, essays,
lectures.   I. Title.
PS121.F57   1986   810'.9   85-22770
ISBN 0-8191-5024-X (alk. paper)
ISBN 0-8191-5025-8 (pbk. : alk. paper)

IN MEMORY OF LEO B. LEVY, 1916-1984,

FRIEND AND COLLEAGUE FOR 25 YEARS

iii

iv

CONTINUITIES: ESSAYS AND IDEAS IN AMERICAN LITERATURE

PREFACE

The essays in this collection stem from more than 30 years of thinking about literature and particularly about American literature in a cultural context. They span a period, the first part of which saw the New Criticism establish the aesthetic and technical principles which emphasized the integrity of the text. The latter part of this period has been marked by the rise of literary theory with an even more exalted conception of textuality, a theory largely separated from history, society, politics, and the realities of human life. The New Critics deepened our sense of structural integrity, organization, and design, and thereby prepared us for that set of different emphases on structuralism, affecting our views of literature, language, and societies. We are now in a post-structuralist period, exposed to the phenomena and asked to assimilate the vocabulary of deconstruction. Both the New Critics and today's theorists wanted to purge the discipline of impressionism and imprecision, to make the study of literature more truly disciplined. But both yesterday's emphasis on the structure of the text and today's deconstructive textuality have denigrated and displaced the history of events, the history of ideas, and the idea of literary history.

A potential student of literature asked to read a contemporary theorist could easily find his interest in literature diminished. A general reader could be forgiven for preferring the aesthetics of Dada to the arguments of Derrida. The genuine analytical benefits of deconstruction would not sufficiently indemnify us if the enterprise were to alienate the potential audience and divert the student interest in literature. Unfortunately, the most dogmatic of literary theorists have little sympathy and less need for other literary approaches or forms of literary criticism, and the practitioners of critical pluralism or of a synthetic and eclectic criticism are too rare. If the effect of deconstructive analysis were the self-destruction of literature's ties to life--to history, philosophy, politics, religion, psychology or the other arts--we would be paying a very high price for its insights. I am not ready to sacrifice contextuality to an exalted emphasis on textuality.

Thus at a time when literary theory and criticism are becoming more highly specialized and recondite, I feel a special need to reassert a critical approach that connects literature to life's more recurrent and compelling questions. We cannot always trust the view that would compel by the weight of novelty and currency, but must seek a second or a third opinion on questions of the human condition. This is an educational and cultural issue of major importance, though many might consider it an isolated academic question or an area of trivial pursuit. It is an issue of major importance because some of our professional directions seem to hasten the demise of the humanities. For the advocates of high-tech "excellence" in our universities, the humanities have already sunk into irrelevance and obscurity. No university on the make considers the humanities seriously. They cannot be glamourized in catalogs and brochures and are generally omitted from the videotaped exercises in self-congratulation that punctuate the halftime lulls of collegiate football games on television. Few, if any, of the myriad workshops for administrators devote any time to the humanities as a dimension of university concern. The humanities are neither a hot issue nor a cool medium.

As we grow long in the tooth and shorter of breath, we learn more of closing coronary arteries, disintegrating discs, and the petrified particles in kidneys or bladders than we ever wanted to know. We go from the art of the film to filmed-over retinas. Once-young poets and scholars of verse cringe at the forms of transverse colons and the unfunny diversions of diverticulosis. Philosophy yields to physiology, and we become scientists against our wills. Yeats' aged man is all too much with us.

Anyone who has spent 30 years as a teacher of literature has seen the ranks of his teachers diminish and the ranks of his colleagues begin to thin. Even the audience for eulogies seems to shrink, and the sense of loss is unrelieved by ceremonial appropriateness because what these forebears and friends lived for and worked at does not seem destined to survive long. The prospect of having to mourn the demise of the humanities intensifies each individual loss and raises the further possibility that the unhappy development might be marked by a dearth of mourners.

Despite this dark prospect, it is too early for funereal surrender; and it is with some hope of asserting the continuity of literary and cultural contextuality and of opposing the insularity and aridity of a pure and socially uncontaminated emphasis on textuality that I offer these essays. All of them deal with ideas, issues, and circumstances that have informed American writing from the time when there was no American identity until the present. The individual essays focus on Hawthorne, Melville, Whitman, and Mark Twain, with questions of class, caste, and race central to the Melville, Whitman, and Twain sections. A question of race, specifically that of Anglo-American and Indian relations, rises again in the concluding essay, which surveys four centuries of American apocalyptic writing. Beginning with the first published history of American settlement (1654), it contains lengthy analyses of works by Joel Barlow, Henry Thoreau, and James Dickey.

In addition to these continuing social questions, there are other factors linking these essays, pervasive continuities far stronger than the occasional discontinuities or contrasts which may appear. In its origins the first essay antedates my encounter with the purposes and personalities of the American Studies doctoral program at Minnesota in the 1950's. I hope that it reflects the solid and serious grounding in literary study received from such Wayne State University figures as Chester Jorgensen, Joseph Prescott, Herb Schueller, Leo Kirschbaum, Orville Linck, Les Dickinson, Dayle Wallace, and Woodburn Ross. In style and argument the opening essay is a conservative contrast to those that follow--essays that illustrate the influence of the program shaped by Tremaine McDowell, Henry Nash Smith, and Leo Marx, and bolstered by Mulford Sibley, Alice Felt Tyler, Bernard Bowron, Donald Torbert, Mary Turpie, May Brodbeck, Clarke Chambers, Joseph Kwiat, David Noble, and (somewhat anomalously) Andreas Papandreou.

But central to that first essay is a conservative concept of humanism linking an American Romantic and an English Neoclassical writer. Despite the formalities of diction and documentation, the essay was an attempt to enlarge the kind of literary exercise that deals in sources and influences. It was an attempt to view the continuity of ideas as being no less important than the discontinuities of culture and politics, to show our

ix

first major fiction writer as being sustained by, even as he was constrained by, "the courtly muses of Europe."

The second essay explores the individual and social circumstances that bring about the humanizing conversion of the narrowly conservative narrator in "Bartleby." Melville's humanism is more subtle and intense than the philosophical abstractions and moral injunctions of the first essay. He challenges the reader's perception to go beyond the limits of circumstance, assumption, and convention and to recognize a web of economic, psychological, artistic, and spiritual implications. The problems of perception and the cultural insularity that intensifies them are even more prominent in the puzzle of "Benito Cereno." This story has proved to be so prophetic and provocative that it has functioned as a kind of literary litmus test for hundreds of critics and thousands of readers and thereby demonstrated how irrevocably subjective critical discourse and interpretation can be.

The Whitman and Mark Twain essays pit vernacular flexibility and functionalism against genteel rigidity and authoritarianism, and link the implications of an organic aesthetic theory to the bio-humanistic core of Pudd'nhead Wilson and its cryptic adherence to the social and psychological integrity of the organism. Both essays on Mark Twain tend to expose the bitterest aspects of American literary self-appraisal. The Whitman essay, however, leans in the opposite direction with a tone that now seems self-congratulatory, perhaps even a bit strident. The reason for this lies not only in the subject matter but also in the fact that it was first written for delivery to foreign audiences.

The final essay, with attention to works of history, poetry, personal narrative, theology, political polemic, fiction, and pop culture, traces the continuities and convolutions of American apocalyptic thought and leads us from visions of messianic salvation to nightmares of secular incineration.

At various times and in varying forms these essays demonstrate what Edward Said has recently termed "cultural affiliation" (The World, The Text, and The Critic, Cambridge, 1983). With a basic respect for the aesthetic and semantic strategies of the text, I have

x

also been concerned with its relation to the author, to other authors, and to other texts; to a historical situation and to readers then and now; to religious and political beliefs; to questions of psychology and personality; to the past, the present, and in so far as possible, the future. These affiliative assumptions underlie what I mean by contextuality.

In volume, more than one-third of this collection is new and heretofore unpublished. "Do Not Bring Your Dog" was delivered as a recent lecture in an NEH sponsored series on Victorian America. "No More Water, The Fire Next Time" was written with the aid of a Huntington Library Fellowship in 1983. Several of the older essays appeared in the _Journal of the History of Ideas_, _The Southern Review_, and the _Platte Valley Review_. The Melville sections appeared in different form in _Going Under: Melville's Short Fiction and The American 1850's_, published by the Louisiana State University Press. I am grateful to the original publishers for permission to use these materials. I hope that their republication here can give them some new meaning and that the cultural and genetic continuities in this collection may serve to strengthen the claims of contextuality in the continuing discussions of textuality and intertextuality.

THE PATTERN OF CONSERVATISM IN JOHNSON'S RASSELAS
AND HAWTHORNE'S TALES

Initially there seems to be little justification for a comparison of Samuel Johnson and Nathaniel Hawthorne; yet the two men shared a set of ideas basic to most of their work. Neither the personal life, the career, nor the literary legacy of Johnson resembles that of Hawthorne. Johnson could never forgive himself for seeking the companionship of the tavern and dominating his company. Hawthorne, on the other hand, regretted his years of solitude and, of course, never reached the dictatorial eminence of Dr. Johnson. Though he fitted no stereotype, Johnson was a Tory in his political sympathies.[1] Hawthorne, however, took part in a socialistic project organized by the Transcendentalists and later shared profitably in the spoils of a Democratic victory.[2] Johnson, although he expanded the limits of neo-classicism in his day, depended heavily on the neo-classical ideals; but Hawthorne's work is integral to American romanticism. Despite all these evident differences, a common pattern of thought pervades the work of these two literary figures--the pattern of conservatism.

Defining conservatism here offers no great difficulty, for I am using it in a general sense and not in reference to any specific political program. Conservatism here means concern with the preservation of traditional human values and the encouragement of moral principles which seem to have endured throughout human experience. The term has reference to a type of world outlook

. . . which turned to the total experience of mankind in the past for guidance in the troubled present; which accepted established institutions as the necessary basis for all social progress; which recognized a body of doctrine built up out of human experience as the surest guide to practice in the present; which valued the trained judgment and discipline of mind and character as the only basis of right living; and which distrusted innovation and the various naturalistic nostrums of the day.[3]

Russell Kirk, one of the ablest spokesmen for conservatism today, would object only to the past tense in this quotation but might offer a few additional characteristics. Among these would be: the "belief that a divine intent rules society as well as conscience"; that true freedom in a civilized society is predicated upon maintenance of class structure and the institutions of property; that the lessons of human experience are prescriptive and constitute the only reasonable check on emotional excess and anarchic impulse; that progress, though possible, is painfully slow, and seldom, if ever, a consequence of innovation or attempt at reform; and that "Providence is the proper instrument for change."[4]

Conservatives, Kirk suggests, are often united by their opposition to certain political and social ideas, most of which he terms principles of radicalism. Thus a conservative would oppose all notions of the perfectibility of man and the progressive improvement of society through education, positive legislation, or alteration of the environment, and affirm instead that humanity has an inherent tendency toward violence and sin. The conservative would object also to neglecting tradition in favor of individual reason, impulse, or materialistic determinism as sufficient guides to social conduct. In addition, he would, of course, oppose total political or economic democracy.[5]

My purpose in this study is not to establish a source for Hawthorne's distrust of the rationalistic reformer or his aversion to the benign faith of the Transcendentalists. Rather I wish to demonstrate that both Johnson and Hawthorne reacted strongly to ideas current in their respective centuries——ideas stemming from a supreme faith in man's malleability——and that their recoil from a supreme faith in optimism of the Enlightenment produced parallel moral contours.

Rasselas embodies the most complete and concise formulation of Johnson's attitudes toward man and society. Here he comes to grips with many of the prevalent ideas of the eighteenth century. Thus I have juxtaposed pertinent themes from _Rasselas_ and ample illustrations from Hawthorne's tales——illustrations which establish the moral kinship of Samuel Johnson and Nathaniel Hawthorne.

Largely as a result of Boswell's descriptions, Johnson was for many years portrayed as the utterer of platitudinous morals and the unswerving advocate of the most rigid combination of authority, reason, and restraint. Recent critics have more wisely dealt with his deep understanding of human nature and the essential validity of more of his literary criticism, less wisely perhaps with his own personal struggles and peculiarities. Hawthorne was also prematurely judged-- but as an artist with a fervid imagination, limitless fancy, too much concern with sin, and with no philosophical permanence. Poe went so far as to caution him to "get a bottle of visible ink" for a change. It is only recently that commentators have become aware of a durability in Hawthorne's writings which stems both from his perception of human nature and from a consciously artistic handling of structural detail and development. Though these early estimates of each writer seem at great variance from each other, it is only because the critics fastened on the most obvious and most extreme characteristics in the works of each man, while ignoring the less obvious but more important ideas.

Hawthorne's relish for the eighteenth century and his literary debt to the proprieties of the Augustan style have been briefly noted by critics.[6] Furthermore, in his response to the social and intellectual currents of his age, he also approximated the view of a considerable segment of eighteenth-century English society--here represented by Samuel Johnson. Since Johnson is hardly peculiar to his age (except for his personality), I claim no unique connection between him and Hawthorne. Instead I suggest that Hawthorne's debt to the eighteenth century extends beyond literary style to include a core of conservative ideas. By first indicating Hawthorne's general impression of Johnson and then using Rasselas as the locus of opinions--on religion, psychology, science, and human conduct-- shared by the two men, I shall explore an important aspect of Hawthorne's intellectual inheritance.

Near the end of his life, Hawthorne in Our Old Home comments on his visit to Johnson's birthplace:

. . . I was but little interested in the legends of the remote antiquity of Lichfield, being drawn thither partly to see its beautiful cathedral, and

3

still more, I believe, because it was the birth-place of Dr. Johnson, with whose sturdy English character I became acquainted, at a very early period of my life, through the good offices of Mr. Boswell. In truth, he seems as familiar to my recollection, and almost as vivid in his personal aspect to my mind's eye, as the kindly figure of my own grandfather . . . it was as a man, a talk-er, and a humorist, that I knew and loved him, appreciating many of his qualities perhaps more thoroughly than I do now, though never seeking to put my instinctive perception of his character into language.[7]

Hawthorne has, however, forgotten an early sketch on Johnson in <u>Biographical Stories</u>[8] and a significant pas-sage in his <u>American Note-Books</u>:

Dr. Johnson's penance in Uttoxetter Market. A man who does penance in what might appear to lookers-on the most glorious and triumphal circumstance of his life. Each circumstance of the career of an apparently successful man to be a penance and torture to him on account of some fundamental error in his early life.[9]

Here is not only an instinctive perception into John-son's character, but also the germinal insight which evolved into the character of Dimmesdale in <u>The Scarlet Letter</u>.[10]

Hawthorne continues his estimate of Johnson:

Beyond all question, I might have had a wiser friend than he. The atmosphere in which alone he breathed was dense; his awful dread of death showed how much muddy imperfection was to be cleansed out of him, before he could be capable of spiritual existence; he meddled only with the surface of life, and never cared to penetrate further than a ploughshare depth; his very sense and sagacity were but a one-eyed clearsightedness. I laughed at him, sometimes, standing beside his knee. And yet, considering that my native propen-sities were towards Fairy Land, and also how much yeast is generally mixed up with the mental suste-nance of a New Englander, it may not have been altogether amiss, in those childish and boyish

days, to keep pace with this heavy-footed travel-
ler, and feed on the gross diet that he carried in
his knapsack. It is wholesome food even now.[11]

Hawthorne goes on to say that what enabled him to enjoy
England and readily to amalgamate English ideas with
"the American ideas that seemed most adverse to them,
may have been derived from, or fostered and kept alive
by, the great English moralist." "Dr. Johnson's morality," he concludes, "was as English an article as a
beefsteak."[12] Hawthorne's trip to Lichfield and
Uttoxetter becomes a pilgrimage as he visits the place
of Johnson's birth and searches for the exact spot
where the aged Dr. Johnson stood penitent in the rain.
And in Notes on Travel, Hawthorne exclaims how gratified he would be if, as a result of his pilgrimage, a
monument were dedicated to Johnson.[13] Truly Johnson
was a giant in Hawthorne's estimation of the eighteenth
century.[14]

Though I am here concerned with the intellectual
relationship between Rasselas and Hawthorne's tales, I
find additional support for this kinship in Hawthorne's
familiarity with the mere details of Rasselas. On the
second page of Fanshawe, he writes of hill country
which is "well-nigh as inaccessible . . . as the Happy
Valley of Abyssinia"[15] (undeniably the home of Johnson's discontented prince), and in an article in The
American Magazine, concludes with this sentence: "Yet
we derive the same moral from the result, as from the
tale of the astronomer, in Rasselas,--that the administration of the Elemental Kingdom would only be changed
for the worse, by the interference of man."[16] Of
course, it is pure chance that Hawthorne thought of
Johnson's astronomer; he did so only because he was
writing an article on lightning rods, which brought to
mind this astronomer who sought to control the weather.
As in the case of Johnson's penance, the moral significance beneath the actual details would linger in Hawthorne's mind, and this moral idea would be reshaped in
an entirely new context.[17]

One of the great problems troubling the eighteenth
century was the ethical question: How should man live?
This was an intensely practical age, and thus required
solutions in the form of reliable guides. The age
wanted, as did Rasselas, a "director in the choice of
life." As a general rule, men still believed in cer-

5

tainty of knowledge. Truth, like natural law, was inherent in the structure of the universe. All man had to do was to employ his divine reason and discover that truth. But some more skeptical men, like Johnson in _Rasselas_, were dubious, in view of the variety of solutions. Johnson did not, of course, deny that man could employ his reason in search of truth. He offered, rather, a necessary corrective for the facile and optimistic answers which many of his contemporaries had so soothingly accepted. Although he valued the lessons of experience, Johnson also rejected the direction taken by Bacon, Berkeley, and Hume; and he was too conservative a Christian to sympathize with the unorthodox ideas of the Deists. Like today's conservative who distrusts any systematic ideology, what troubled Johnson was not only the answer, but also the way in which the answer was reached. His antagonism was directed at all forms of shoddy thinking which pretended to cure the world of its ills. Many eighteenth-century intellectuals felt that a supernatural revelation of religious or ethical truth was unnecessary, that the physical universe was itself a perfect revelation of God, and that man was naturally good and perfectible through external means. The mood ranged from rationalism to sentimentalism, from cool analysis to enthusiastic feeling, from optimism of acceptance to optimism of progress; but it stemmed from a single tendency: a supreme faith in nature. Johnson opposed this tendency. In everything he examined, in everything he did, Johnson always insisted on "a bottom of common sense" and everything in _Rasselas_, everything in Samuel Johnson, bears the mark of this "common sense."

Prominent among the panaceas offered the eighteenth century was Jean-Jacques Rousseau's remedy for an ailing society. Both Rousseau and Johnson tried to tell their age how to live—a task made more difficult by the transitional nature of the age. Though Johnson staunchly denied it, conservative Toryism was giving way to a new vision of man and society, a vision which would pervade the nineteenth century. But Johnson could not agree with Rousseau that man's environment—his habits, customs, and institutions—was responsible for the evil in man, and expressed only irritation and contempt at the Frenchman's ideas.

Throughout the volumes of Boswell's _Life_, Johnson denounces Rousseau as a dealer in paradoxes, a childish seeker after novelty, a public menace, a bare-faced writer of nonsense, a charlatan who laughed at the world for taking him seriously, and above all, a rascal who ought to be hunted out of society.[18] The good doctor felt that Rousseau's radical doctrines were a dangerous challenge to the supremacy of reason, that the state of nature was actually a state of animal imbecility. When Rasselas, in the course of his travels, meets with simple shepherds, who live a primitive life outside the bounds of civilization, he finds that these shepherds in their ignorance can communicate little more than their discontent. Johnson's refutation of Rousseau may not seem very fair; but because Rousseau's cure belonged to Johnson's category of shoddy thinking, he chose the most direct attack.

To counteract those who betrayed the classical virtues of judgment, reason, and good sense, Johnson approached the ethical question with these assumptions: Man is born to suffer; externals, institutions, social agencies, do not affect human happiness, for this happiness is the product of individual discipline and outlook. Happiness, if it exists, is to be found in the ability to accept the few joys while enduring the numerous miseries of life. "The only practicable reform is that which is aimed at individual human nature through moral persuasion and encouragement, or at the most a few private charities and the righting of local wrongs. Radical changes, or changes en masse, would very probably make things even worse than they are."[19] He felt, as did Hawthorne, that the result of organized reform would threaten the already tottering basis of civilization and could bring the whole social structure into a state of moral and constitutional anarchy. Johnson's own pessimism brings him closer to Rousseau than he ever imagined. Both men had a sense of justice and a strong feeling for humanity, but Johnson felt Rousseau's schemes to be corrupted at their source and fraught with potential disaster--not merely primitivism, but barbarism.

Like Johnson in Rasselas, Hawthorne employs a fictional framework to offer a social corrective in the "Earth's Holocaust." Concentrating on the Rousseauistic concept, Hawthorne uses the purifying influence of a ravenous fire to attempt the eradication of the numerous institutions which have become responsible for the perversion of man's nature. Hurled into the con-

7

suming fire are all the pedigrees of aristocratic families, the badges of monarchs and nobility, the weapons of war, the instruments of capital punishment, money, books (which constitute "dead men's thoughts"), and all the trappings of religion. But will man now be able to start anew and avoid the evils which had bound him? Hawthorne states his position:

> How sad a truth, if true it were, that man's age-long endeavor for perfection had served only to render him the mockery of the evil principle, from the fatal circumstance of an error at the very root of the matter! The heart, the heart,-- there was the little yet boundless sphere wherein the original wrong of which the crime and misery of this outward world were merely types. Purify that inward sphere, and the many shapes of evil that haunt the outward, and which now seem almost our only realities, will burn to shadowy phantoms and vanish of their own accord; but if we go no deeper than the intellect, and strive, with merely that feeble instrument, to discern and rectify what is wrong, our whole accomplishment will be a dream, so unsubstantial that it matters little whether the bonfire, which I have so faithfully described, were what we choose to call a real event and a flame that would scorch the finger, or only a phosphoric radiance and a parable of my own brain.[20]

What Johnson set out to accomplish through disillusioned but restrained satire, Hawthorne effects with a reduction of the problem to its crux of emotional horror. Hawthorne's common sense, derived from experience, informed him that the fault was within man more often than in the externals of society. Rousseau had made no provision for purifying the heart of man, for moral reform within the individual. He believed, rather, that man was innately good, and that with the elimination of institutions which distorted basic human nature, the goodness would assert itself.

In their insistence that man cannot improve himself by wholesale destruction of social institutions, both Johnson and Hawthorne follow a traditional antithesis of intellect and passions. For Hawthorne, man's moral judgment is a result of an interaction of head and heart. Even though the heart could at times re-

8

spond intuitively to truth, it is only from the cooperation of head and heart that the bulk of the valid moral standards are derived. Every effort of man must be to balance these antithetical forces to achieve any semblance of life's potential happiness. But Hawthorne feels that the head is too apt to upset this delicate balance and is not to be trusted. This destruction of man's equilibrium through workings of the intellect forms one of Hawthorne's recurrent theses and gives rise to the Unpardonable Sin.[21]   Ethan Brand's shortcoming was the sin of an intellect that dominated the more instinctive and heartfelt sense of brotherhood with man and reverence for God. Ethan Brand is insane, a horrible fiend, for his heart has atrophied, and as Hawthorne says, "his moral nature had ceased to keep pace of improvement with his intellect." For Hawthorne the heart has more sway over the will than has the mind.[22]

On this score Johnson, too, is very outspoken. One of his fundamental convictions was that "the structure of the universe and the essential nature of man are so overwhelmingly the most important factors in determining the good and evil of the human lot as to render climate, government or social institutions secondary at best and insufficient in themselves to do more than make it somewhat better or somewhat worse."[23] Perhaps because he was closer to the Renaissance and historical humanist tradition, Johnson felt that the intelligence was man's noblest endowment and was to be elevated over the lower faculties of the emotions: "that wherever human nature is to be found, there is a mixture of vice and virtue, a contest of passion and reason; and that the creator doth not appear partial in his distributions, but has balanced, in most countries their particular inconveniences by particular favors."[24]   Because the reader may here be concerned about Hawthorne's trust in the "heart" and Johnson's trust in the "intellect," I should point out that what Johnson terms "intellect" and Hawthorne "heart" ultimately fulfill many of the same functions, but for Hawthorne the heart, that "inward sphere," lies deeper than the intellect. The intellect meant to Johnson not only the force governing man's logical activities but also his spiritual nature, his will, and it is an act of the intelligence that dictates:

Yet, when the sense of sacred presence fires,
And strong devotion to the skies aspires,
Pour forth thy fervours for a healthful mind,
Obedient passions, and a will resign'd . . .[25]

Johnson's belief in the necessary balance between
thinking and feeling in art as in life led him to censure Dryden, whose work he largely admired, for not
exhibiting "the genuine operations of the heart."[26]
Concerning Dryden he wrote:

The power that predominated in his intellectual
operations, was rather strong reason than quick
sensibility. Upon all occasions that were presented, he studied rather than felt, and produced
sentiments not such as nature enforces, but medi-
tation supplies.[27]

Thus it was that both Johnson and Hawthorne believed in the necessary maintenance of social institutions built up out of human experience as well as
discipline of head and heart as a prerequisite for
right living. Johnson, who hated both pedants and
scientists who had become too much enveloped in their
specialized studies, anticipated Hawthorne's concept of
a misdirected intellect--his Unpardonable Sin.

In the light of the dualistic psychology which
Hawthorne employed, his attitudes toward reform and
reformers became clarified. It was not the principle
of reform but the method of the zealous reformer which
disturbed Hawthorne. Like Johnson, Hawthorne could
never deny a beggar, but the professional mendicant or
organized charity received his disdain. The social
reformer, who though his goal be admirable, pursues his
single idea or theory to the exclusion of all spiritual
development, becomes as unbalanced, as isolated, as
perverted as does Chillingworth. His head has shut out
his heart, and for Hawthorne there is no greater human
tragedy. In his American Note-Books Hawthorne devises
a plot in which a reformer, on the point of making converts to his extreme doctrines, is discovered to be a
fugitive from a madhouse,[28] and in "The Procession of
Life" he speaks of the charitable man whose heart may
be large, but whose mind "is often of such moderate
dimensions as to be exclusively filled up with one
idea."

When a good man has long devoted himself to a particular kind of beneficence--to one species of
reform--he is apt to become narrowed into the
limits of the path wherein he treads and to fancy
that there is no other good to be done on earth
but that selfsame good to which he has put his
hand, and in the very mode that best suits his own
conceptions.[29]

Johnson, as we shall see, makes an even more detailed
analysis of the monomaniac, exhibiting the same attitudes as Hawthorne toward any man who deviates from the
prescribed norms of human conduct.

Rousseau's panacea was, of course, not the only
remedy which Johnson was compelled to challenge. He
could not overlook any system which seemed to deny the
truths of human experience. Early in the tale of
Rasselas, before the prince has escaped the sensual
plenty of his Happy Valley, Johnson aims his criticism
at a species of benevolism which underlay much of the
optimistic thought of the eighteenth century.
Rasselas, aware that man may suffer misery and dis-
tress, finds that his suffering and the enjoyment of
that suffering can be co-existent. Johnson characterizes Rasselas in this state of mind as a "man of feeling" who is able "to feel some complacence in his own
perspicacity, and to receive some solace of the miseries of life, from consciousness of the delicacy with
which he felt, and the eloquence with which he bewailed
them."[30]

Johnson's target here is the Narcissus-like complacency achieved by the followers of benevolism, men
who believed in the doctrine of man's innate virtue and
philanthropy. The benevolists in full seriousness
could declare that the more eloquent the display of
emotion, the more admirable the person. This very
explicit attack on Shaftesbury, who is one of
Rousseau's sources, becomes more pronounced when
Rasselas, raising his eyes to the mountain which hindered his flight from the Happy Valley, exclaims, "This
. . . is the fatal obstacle that hinders, at once, the
enjoyment of pleasure, and the exercise of virtue."[31]

But this is not Johnson's only directed attack on
the facile optimism of his day. Rasselas, soon after
his departure from the Happy Valley, meets the only man

who will consent to advise him in the "choice of life." This man, a philosopher, explained that "the way to be happy is to live according to nature, in obedience to that universal and unalterable law, with which every heart is originally impressed."[32] This, and his further dictum "that deviation from nature is deviation from happiness," sounded very attractive to the earnest young prince. Upon further inquiry as to what it is to live according to nature, the sage expounded:

> 'To live according to nature, is to act always with due regard to the fitness arising from the relations and qualities of causes and effects; to concur with the great and unchangeable scheme of universal felicity; to cooperate with the general disposition and tendency of the present system of things.'

> The prince soon found that this was one of the sages whom he should understand less, as he heard him longer. He, therefore, bowed, and was silent, and the philosopher, supposing him satisfied, and the rest vanquished, rose and departed, with the air of a man that had cooperated with the present system.[33]

Johnson felt that the growing strength of this naturalistic school presented a much more subtle danger, undermining, as it did, the foundations of reason and the lessons of experience. These philosophers, notably Shaftesbury and Rousseau, have not enough of the substance of reality to irritate Johnson; so rather than elaborating on their mistaken beliefs, he translates their set of ideas into philosophical doubletalk.

The climate of ideas presented by these benevolent optimists and naturalistic philosophers is not wholly unlike what Hawthorne encountered a hundred years later in the maxims of Emerson and his fellow Transcendentalists. What Johnson objected to in the Deism of Shaftesbury and Bolingbroke, Hawthorne criticized in nineteenth-century Transcendentalism and Unitarianism. In the very places that Emerson perceived potential divinity, under the most spotless and respected reputations, Hawthorne discovered secret sins and vague impulses to evil. Emerson's assuring philosophy was to Hawthorne a construct of vaporous unrealities; Emerson is "that everlasting rejector of all that is, and seeker for he knows not what."[34] Hawthorne's skeptical view of reformers, too, was that they could not grasp reality and overrated that natural virtue of man.

In "The Celestial Railroad" Hawthorne borrows from Bunyan, whom Johnson praised highly,[35] to satirize the new way to salvation. Men may now be comfortable as they travel to heaven via railroad. They can laugh as they swiftly pass the plodding pilgrim, Christian, who follows the old road to salvation. Guide on the celestial railroad is Mr. Smooth-it-away, who points out a convenient bridge which has a base made of "some editions of books of morality; volumes of French philosophy and German rationalism; tracts, sermons, and essays of modern clergymen; extracts from Plato, Confucius, and various Hindoo sages, together with a few ingenious commentaries upon texts of scripture,--all of which, by some scientific process, have been converted into a mass like granite."[36] Moreover, the passengers need not carry their burdens of sin, for a baggage car has been provided--to the delight of the various passengers, Mr. Smooth-it-away, Mr. Live-for-the-world, Mr. Hide-sin-in-the-heart, Mr. Scaly-conscience, and citizens of the town Shun-Repentance.

The travellers then reach a cavern wherein dwells a terrible giant who seizes upon honest passers-by and fattens them on meals of smoke, mist, moonshine, raw potatoes, and sawdust. His name is, of course, Giant Transcendentalist, but his physical description is exceedingly vague. He shouts after the travellers "but in so strange a phraseology that we knew not what he meant, nor whether to be encouraged or affrighted."[37] Beyond this obstacle is Vanity Fair, a very respectable place, full of Unitarian ministers and transcendentalist lecturers, a place where erudition may be got without even learning to read. Thus Hawthorne progresses to the ironic conclusion of his tale: the two pilgrims travelling on foot reach the celestial city, but those on the train remain on the outside looking in.[38]

The principle is much the same as Johnson felt: there is no easy way to virtue, no comfortable way to salvation, no ready-made nourishment for the spirit. Both men condemned the exponents of too facile or too optimistic a religion which promised heaven for everyone because each man has natural divinity inherent in him. In each instance, the spokesman for the easy way is made to speak in incomprehensible, vague, philosophical gibberish.

Extremes of sensual indulgence or of stoic repression, though certainly not new to the eighteenth century, still represented for some a feasible refuge from worldly discomfort. When Rasselas joins the company of young men "whose only business is to gratify their desires, and whose time is all spent in a succession of enjoyments," he soon realizes the futility of trying to satisfy man's fleeting desires and turns away in disgust.

> Their mirth was without images; their laughter without motive; their pleasures were gross and sensual, in which the mind had no part; their conduct was, at once, wild and mean; they laughed at order and at law, but the frown of power dejected, and the eye of wisdom abashed them.

> The prince soon concluded, that he should never be happy in a course of life of which he was ashamed.[39]

Contrastingly, Rasselas next inquires of the life of rigor. The ideal of the Stoics appealed to many in Johnson's age because of the emphasis placed on reason. Rasselas hears how dangerous are the emotions--those lower faculties which can so readily dominate the mind. After learning the formulas for subduing passion, Rasselas returns to Imlac, convinced that he has found "a man who can teach all that is necessary to be known." This man is immovable by pain and pleasure, indifferent to the accidents which men term good and evil, and sits on the "unshaken throne of rational fortitude."

He is unable, therefore, to accept Imlac's acrid, but well-grounded retort: "Be not too hasty . . . to trust, or to admire the teachers of morality: they discourse, like angels, but they live, like men." Not until he sees the philosopher lamenting the death of his only daughter, the comfort of his old age, does Rasselas perceive the emptiness of the Stoic's polished rhetoric. The sage wails that all the truth and reason can do for him now is to tell him that his daughter cannot be restored.[40] Johnson thus broke with the rigorists when he calmly recognized that, whatever the effects, the instincts and emotions, because they are ineradicable, have to be tolerated. They are part of human nature.

Hawthorne adopts a similar view of man's essential dualism. In "The Maypole of Merry Mount" he pictures two distinct types of life--the joyous, unrestrained revelling of the Merry Mounters, who cater to the _passions_ of the heart, and the strict rational life of the Puritans, who restrain the whims of the heart with their _intellects_. Hawthorne intends the Merry Mounters to represent the victims of "Erring Thought and perverted Wisdom."[41] They have so overindulged in "a wild philosophy of pleasure" that their senses have been jaded; the "fresh gayety" of their hearts has been lost. Rebelling against any taint of the intellect, they refuse to allow their heads to lead them "among the sober truths of life not even to be truly blest."[42]

The Puritans, however, labor between the prayers of dawn and dusk, and upon assembling, they seek no mirth. Stern, grave, deliberate, they listen to ponderous sermons. Suppressing the heart, they reason out everything according to divine law. Opposed to the Merry Mounters, who "laugh at order and at law," the Puritans stand for a rational approach to life and a Stoic suppression of the feelings.

Enmeshed in the conflict between these two incompatible ideas are the Lord and Lady of the May. About to be married when Endicott and his Puritan band come on the scene and stem the revelry, the two young people stand between the two opposing life forces. To the two who are in love, the onslaught of the dark Puritan and his rational life is beneficial, for they are able to effect a balance between the two excesses of human life. Love, the purest expression of the heart, is combined with the complementary elements of the head, and the result is the realization that life has responsibilities to complement its revelries. Unlike either of the extremes, these two young people will have a soul undamaged by preponderance of head or heart, and this is Hawthorne's point: that any imbalance in man's nature will leave its mark on the soul and consequently on the prospect of immortality. Johnson would agree without qualification.

15

Another aspect of the dangers involved in allowing an imbalance of head and heart is revealed in both Johnson's and Hawthorne's treatment of the scientist: he is a man whose head has taken precedence over his heart. Not to be overlooked, also, is the explicit denial of science as a progressive factor in man's betterment of himself or his environment.

When Rasselas declares his intention to devote his life to science and solitude, Imlac's stabilizing comments must return the prince to the middle road of life. Imlac tells of his acquaintance with a most learned astronomer who has devoted forty years of undivided energy in calculation and study of the celestial bodies.[43] Though isolated, this scientist has not been so perverted that he can no longer claim the brotherhood of mankind, but yet, contrary to Rasselas' supposition, he is not happy. Unwilling to discuss the blessings which he is believed to enjoy, he invariably changes the subject, appearing uneasy and confused.

Something is obviously troubling this man, something that is not common or natural to ordinary men, else he would not be so reluctant to speak. Imlac soon learns the secret, for the old man tells him that he has long discharged an office which he wishes Imlac to continue: he has regulated the weather and distributed the seasons, manipulated the stars and controlled the waters. Only the winds refuse to obey him.[44] Furthermore he is the first who has been entrusted with such power, but he finds himself far less happy than before because of the "weariness of unremitted vigilance." This condition, then, is a result of the unvarying and relentless pursuit of scientific fact. And it is this condition, this very instance, to which Hawthorne referred in The American Magazine when he wrote that "the administration of the Elemental Kingdom would only be changed for the worse, by the interference of man."

Finding nothing ludicrous in this astronomer's obsessions, Imlac echoes Johnson's own sentiment on madness. Gravely Imlac says:

Few can attain this man's knowledge, and few practise his virtues; but all may suffer his calamity. Of the uncertainties of our present state, the

most dreadful and alarming is the uncertain con-
tinuance of reason. . . .

Disorders of the intellect . . . happen much
more often than superficial observers will easily
believe. Perhaps, if we speak with rigorous
exactness, no human mind is in its right state.
There is no man, whose imagination does not, sometimes, predominate over his reason, who can regu-
late his attention wholly by his will, and whose
ideas will come and go at his command. No man
will be found, in whose mind airy notions do not,
sometimes, tyrannize, and force him to hope or
fear beyond the limits of sober probability. All
power of fancy over reason, is a degree of insanity; but, while this power is such as we can control and repress, it is not visible to others, nor
considered as any depravation of the mental faculties; it is not pronounced madness, but when it
comes ungovernable, and apparently influences
speech or action.

To indulge the power of fiction, and send
imagination out upon the wing, is often the sport
of those who delight too much in silent speculation. . . .

In time, some particular train of ideas fixes
the attention; all other intellectual gratifica-
tions are rejected; the mind, in weariness or
leisure, recurs constantly to the favourite conception, and feasts on the luscious falsehood,
whenever she is offended with the bitterness of
truth. By degrees, the reign of fancy is con-
firmed; she grows first imperious, and in time
despotick. Then fictions begin to operate as
realities, false opinions fasten upon the mind,
and life passes in dreams of rapture or of an-
guish.

This, sir, is one of the dangers of solitude,
which the hermit has confessed not always to promote goodness, and the astronomer's misery has
proved to be not always propitious to wisdom.45

This quotation reads like a check-list of Hawthorne's major themes. Imlac says that such unbalance
in an individual "confers upon his pride unattainable

dominion," and Hawthorne demonstrates the thesis in tale after tale. He writes stories of men whose rationality is seduced by pride in orthodoxy, by pride in speculation, and pride in their detachment from contending parties and schools of thought. In this group are found the Pyncheons, Rappaccini, Aylmer, Chillingworth, Ethan Brand, Richard Digby, Roderick Elliston-- all who turn their backs completely on mankind. Their hearts become stone; their souls wither in their isolation. And all these distorted individuals are categorized by the unnatural scope of their unattainable goals. Insanity, no matter what form, is completely described in terms of the head-heart psychology, and both men find the scientist in his isolation especially prone to this danger.

For example, in "The Birthmark" Aylmer is an eminent scientist in love with his beautiful wife. His devotion to the sciences, however, precludes his ever being "weaned from them by any second passion." A zealous perfectionist, he decides to remove a birthmark, shaped like a miniature hand, from his wife's cheek. Georgiana was so beautiful that this one blemish, so magnified in Aylmer's mind, caused him to forget that this "was the fatal flaw of humanity which Nature, in one shape or another, stamps ineffaceably on all her productions, either to imply that they are temporary and finite, or that their perfection must be wrought by toil and pain."[46]

His single-minded fixation destroys the delicate balance of his two loves, that of science and that of spiritual affinity with another human being, and Aylmer becomes possessed of only one idea: ". . . it so connected itself with innumerable trains of thought and modes of feeling that it became the central point of all."[47] It is as Imlac's diagnosis: ". . . some particular train of ideas fixes the attention. . . ." Aylmer's head and heart no longer operate in equilibrium; all his faculties have coalesced into a consuming and unnatural desire. And like the astronomer who wished to improve on the seasons, Aylmer's intentions are not for evil, but nevertheless they do transgress the powers delegated to man.

Aylmer is not unaware of this singular obsession which gives him no rest. Even when he suspects the awful consequence of his proposed action, he cannot dispel "the tyrannizing influence acquired by one idea over his mind." He has set his goal of perfectibility and is concerned only with attaining it. His fancy has begun to exhibit power over his reason. He plans to seclude himself and his wife in his extensive laboratory, where he has made many great discoveries concerning the heavens, the earth, and the secrets of biology and physiology. He has even tried to duplicate nature in creating life, but has been forced to lay aside this attempt

> . . . in unwilling recognition of the truth—against which all seekers sooner or later stumble—that our great creative Mother, while she amuses us with apparently working in the broadest sunshine, is yet severely careful to keep her own secrets, and, in spite of her pretended openness, shows us nothing but results. <u>She permits us, indeed, to mar, but seldom to mend, and, like a jealous patentee, on no account to make</u>.[48]

With the aid of his shaggy, begrimed helper, Aminadab, Aylmer begins his labors. The brute and intellect, extreme aspects of man's nature, here join in an attempt to improve on Nature's creation.

Georgiana has remained faithful and trusting because of her deeply rooted spiritual love for Aylmer. But in return, she mistakes his concentrated application for holy love when it has actually become an unshakable monomania. Her gentle and devoted nature leads to her death:

> As the last crimson tint of the birthmark—that sole token of human imperfection—faded from her cheek, the parting breath of now perfect woman passed into the atmosphere, and her soul, lingering a moment near her husband, took its heavenward flight. . . . Thus ever does the gross fatality of earth exult in its invariable triumph over the immortal essence which, <u>in this dim sphere of half development, demands the completeness of a higher state</u>. Yet, had Aylmer reached a profounder wisdom, he need not thus have flung away the happiness which would have woven his mortal life of the selfsame texture with the celestial. The momentary circumstance was too strong for him; <u>he</u>

19

<u>failed to look beyond the shadowy scope of time,
and, living once for all in eternity, to find the
perfect future in the present.</u>49

In the same manner that Johnson concludes <u>Rasselas</u>
and "The Vanity of Human Wishes," Hawthorne concludes
his tale of a man prepossessed by science in "The
Birthmark." Aylmer's fanatical attempt to vie with
Nature blinds him to the impossibility of earthly perfection. Hawthorne proposes that only in the after-
world does there exist perfection--and genuine happiness. Such immortality is granted Georgiana by virtue
of her true love, but Aylmer, whose intellectual pride
has unbalanced his nature and distorted his view of
time, remains a didactic and tragic example of intellectual monomania. Had he reached a profounder wisdom,
he might have seen:

These goods for man the laws of heaven ordain;
These goods he grants, who grants the pow'r to
gain;
With these celestial wisdom calms the mind
And makes the happiness she does not find.50

Hawthorne's men of science were seldom redeemable;
Johnson had been somewhat more charitable, for he allowed his astronomer to regain his balance and to diag-
nose his own case:

I have passed my time in study, without experience; in the attainment of sciences, which can,
for the most part, be but <u>remotely useful to man-
kind</u>. . . . If I have obtained any prerogatives
above other students, they have been accompanied
with fear, disquiet, and scrupulosity. . . . I
have suffered much, and suffered it in vain.51

Pleased by the redemption of this wise man, Imlac de-
velops a psychological notion which becomes central to
many of Hawthorne's tales, especially those dealing
with the extremes of the Puritan mind:

No disease of the imagination . . . is so
difficult of cure, as that which is complicated
with the dread of guilt; fancy and conscience then
act interchangeably upon us, and so often shift
their places, that the illusions of one are not
distinguished from the dictates of the other. If

fancy presents images not normal or religious, the mind drives them away when they give it pain, <u>but when melancholick notions take the form of duty, they lay hold on the faculties without opposition, because we are afraid to exclude or banish them</u>. For this reason, the superstitious are often melancholy, and the melancholy always superstitious.[52]

Having in effect disclosed the genesis of Hawthorne's Black Man and the germ of such stories as "Young Goodman Brown" or "The Minister's Black Veil," Imlac continues in a fashion not unlike Hawthorne's concept of a negative democracy in which all men share in sin and guilt.

Keep this thought always prevalent, that you are only one atom of the mass of humanity, and have neither such virtue nor vice, as that you should be singled out for supernatural favours or afflictions.[53]

Young Goodman Brown's vision of a hidden and universal evil or the Reverend Mr. Hooper's obsession with the blackness deep in the hearts of his fellow men, <u>as well as in himself</u>, illustrates Johnson's diagnosis of this "disease of the imagination . . . complicated with the dread of guilt." Johnson's astronomer, "suffering chimeras to prey upon me in secret," is of the species that breeds Hawthorne's moral chiaroscuro.

"When melancholick notions take the form of duty," when an individual concentrates too intensely upon sin, a perversion of basic human nature results. Goodman Brown, honest and devout Christian, after a vision or an actual experience during which he recognizes the sinful nature of all his loved ones, loses faith in his wife and in mankind. Realizing that all around him are sinners and unheedful of the words of the dark figure in the forest that even sinners must depend on the hearts of their fellow men, Goodman isolates himself. He grows stern, sad, meditating in the darkness of a mind that knows only morbid thoughts and allows him to admit only the evil in man. His "disease of the imagination is so difficult of cure" that when he dies, "they carved no hopeful verse upon his tombstone, for his dying hour was gloom."[54]

The Reverend Mr. Hooper, who dons "The Minister's Black Veil" to dramatize the inner secrets of man, is also overconscious of sin. His obsession is, as Johnson analyzed it, "complicated with the dread of guilt." He mistakes all the private matters of his individuality as manifestations of concealed sin. Because he projects his own morbid fancy, he sees every visage a facsimile of his own dismal mask. Like Goodman Brown, the minister's purpose is to isolate himself from the loathsome evils which he has discovered in all men. Thus his veil creates an impenetrable barrier not only between him and his congregation but between him and all men. He is shackled "in that saddest of all prisons, his own heart."[55]

The pattern of conservatism in these two men is almost complete. They have rejected all optimistic or naturalistic faiths which seek to replace formal religion, and they have shown how human nature can be distorted through extremes of restraint, through single-minded devotion to science or through guilt-ridden, melancholy obsessions.

Important to any discussion of conservative philosophy is man's attitude toward the past, the present, and the prospect of immortality. In the humanist tradition, Dr. Johnson recognized that the accumulated experience of the past constituted the best foundation for a judgment of the present. In his advice to Rasselas, Imlac says that man must look to the past for a measuring stick of motives and effects. The past is an extremely useful chronicle; moreover, no part of history is so useful as that which chronicles the progress of the human mind, the development of reason, science, and the arts. This history of ideas, Imlac asserts, is also a means to some semblance of happiness, for a wider range affords the mind more pleasure.[56]

In a famous passage Imlac tells us that the poet "does not number the streaks of the tulip" but describes more general features and more important issues. He must

. . . trace the changes of the human mind, as they are modified by various institutions, and accidental influences. . . . He must divest himself of the prejudices of his age or country; he must con-

sider right and wrong in their abstracted and in-
variable state; he must disregard present laws and
opinions, and rise to general and transcendental
truths, which will always be the same. . . . He
must write, as the interpreter of nature, and the
legislator of mankind, and consider himself, as
presiding over the thoughts and manners of future
generations; as a being superior to time and
place.[57]

In very similar terms, the late F. O. Matthiessen no-
ticed and described Hawthorne's use of the past:

The importance of that sense for an artist is that
by it alone can he escape from mere contempora-
neity, from the superficial and journalistic aber-
rations of the moment, and come into possession of
the primary attributes of man, through grasping
the similarities of his problems beneath differing
guises. The historical sense puts no premium on
the past over the present; it betrays a writer if
it lets him forget the tensions of his own day;
its value lies in increasing his power to concentrate on what is essentially human.[58]

Hawthorne's sense of the past, most evident in his
introductory essay to The Scarlet Letter, underlay many
of his tales. In "The Gray Champion" Hawthorne suggests symbolically that the past is not dead, that the
past has moral value for the present and the future.[59]
Set in New England in 1689, the story deals with the
tyranny of Sir Edmund Andros, who has denied the colonists their civil and religious rights. Dismayed and
frightened by Andros' parade of armed might, the colonists implore Providence for help. Like a manifesta-
tion from heaven, an old man takes his stand in front
of the procession and orders the governor to halt.
This is the unknown Gray Champion who stops the display
of military power and disappears. Not long after,
William of Orange assumes control and Andros' tyranni-
cal administration is abolished.

But Hawthorne shifts from this central experience
of the past to other levels of time. He refers to the
conditions not of the settlers but of the poor and op-
pressed in Britain in his own day,[60] then proceeds to
the future to recall both past and present:

23

But should domestic tyranny oppress us, or the invader's step pollute our soil, still may the Gray Champion come, for he is the type of New England's hereditary spirit; and his shadowy march, on the eve of danger, must ever be the pledge, that New England's sons will vindicate their ancestry.[61]

The Gray Champion has become a symbol of the moral force which deposed a tyrant in England (Charles I), spoke against tyranny in New England in 1689, reappeared in 1770 and in 1775 to vindicate the traditional rights of American colonists, and which will reappear in the future to protest undue oppression by any government. The moral value of the past has thus been dramatized for all time.

Both men, then, utilize the lessons of the past not as a field of study, but as factors of human experience which can be made to function for the benefit of man in the present. An awareness of one's own age, however, is far more necessary than a sterile account of the past which avoids basic human motivations and is too enveloped in a narrowly historical approach. A knowledge of life should be the scholar's goal, and both Johnson and Hawthorne concur that books without the knowledge of life are useless. Johnson insists on "knowledge of the world fresh from life, not strained through books,"[62] and faced with the same issue, Hawthorne asks, ". . . is not Nature better than a book? Is not the human heart deeper than any system of philosophy?"[63]

Man's conduct in the present, in the opinion of these two men, must never be slighted, for certainly his conduct here and now determines his attainment of happiness eventually. In his earthly life, Johnson and Hawthorne concur, no man may rightly achieve happiness, and it is vanity, or error, to try. Even good acts can assure no man of earthly happiness. Rasselas, in his investigation of modes of life, found the prosperous man unhappy because property put his life in danger and put friendship on the peculiar basis of pecuniary favors. The poor man was no less unhappy, for he believed that the rich man delighted in exploiting him. Human nature has been perverted again by a single obsession.

24

When Imlac and Rasselas wonder at the vast chambers of an awesome pyramid, Imlac suggests that its chambers offer neither sufficient protection from an enemy nor the best storage for treasure. It must have been built to gratify the desires of the most vain who are amused by the tedious labor of thousands and who want to publicize their own importance. It is an attempt to secure an earthly immortality through a more durable symbol than the human clay. Imlac concludes with an admonition to man to "Survey the pyramids, and confess thy folly."[64]

Hawthorne tells the tale of "The Ambitious Guest" who seems normal except for an unnatural desire for personal fame and earthly immortality. Not as extreme a violator of Christian brotherhood as Ethan Brand, he is, nevertheless, an isolated individual because of his all-engrossing ambition to be known by posterity, to achieve his monument. Around this single individual, Hawthorne focuses the varying ambitions of the members of the family who befriended him, but none so lofty, so exalted as the aspirations of the young man. The wishes of the family remain unfulfilled, for the entire brood including the young stranger are buried under tons of rock in a landslide. Ironically, the only wish granted is that of the youth who desired a monument of earthly magnificence—but it is a nameless sepulchre. Significantly, Hawthorne's attitude and moral statement echo Johnson's "The Vanity of Human Wishes," and even more of a parallel is seen in the statement:

> Statesmen and warriors and poets have spent their strength in no better cause than this . . . spelling out one's name in the sands of a beach. Return, then, in an hour or two and seek for this mighty record of a name. The sea will have swept over it, even as time rolls its effacing waves over the names of statesmen and warriors and poets.[65]

The classes or professions in this quotation coincide exactly with the sequence in Johnson's poem, and the sentiment is undeniably the same: No mortal act can ever assure any man of immortality, for immortality is not of this world and is not subject to any earthly means.

25

If happiness is so elusive a condition and if man can look forward only to death, need he then despair? Johnson and Hawthorne again provide a similar answer. Let us look again to Imlac, who, stimulated by the Egyptians' attempt to elude death through preserving the body, discourses on the immateriality and eternal duration of the soul. His logic is convincing and his listeners, whose problem has been "the choice of life" and the pursuit of happiness, answer that "the choice of life is become less important," and they think now "on the choice of eternity."66

Such thoughts are native to Hawthorne's tales, and one story, termed by Hawthorne an apologue, concludes in much the same manner as Rasselas. Following the pattern of conservatism, Hawthorne in "The Lily's Quest" also depicts a pursuit of happiness. Two lovers, Adam Forrester and Lilias Fay, search for a suitable place to built their "Temple of Happiness." Adam is griefstricken when his beloved Lily (Lilias) dies, and decides to bury her in their Temple of delight. When the digging was started, it was discovered that beneath their temple lay an ancient sepulchre, and Adam is confronted with the fact that the foundation for their happiness was a grave.

Like Rasselas, who has his insight into eternal truth while standing in the "Mansions of the dead," Adam Forrester suddenly has a vision of hope: "'Joy! joy!' he cried, throwing his arms towards heaven, 'on a grave be the site of our Temple and now our happiness is for Eternity!'"67

Thus the key word "eternity" unlocks the enigma in each instance. Each of these writers "Counts death kind nature's signal of retreat," the only attainable form of happiness for even the noblest of men. Hawthorne himself sums up the philosophy of "The Lily's Quest"--and Rasselas--in a passage placed in his English notes right below a discussion of an event in Johnson's life:

God himself cannot compensate us for being born, in any period short of eternity. All the misery we endure here constitutes a claim for another life;--and, still more, all the happiness, because all true happiness. involves something more

26

than the earth owns and something more than a mortal capacity for the enjoyment of it.[68]

All the fashionable solutions for happy living have been shown in a light that makes them appear of the species Pollyanna rather than truly realistic schemes. At the conclusion of _Rasselas_, each character, like the characters in _Candide_, must cultivate his own garden, but not in a manner that would include withdrawal or solitude. This is not the best of all possible worlds nor is all that occurs therein for the best, and Johnson does not surrender his realistic skepticism to the banal though appealing optimism of his contemporaries. Hawthorne, in the nineteenth century, testifies to the validity of Johnson's conclusions.

From this lengthy comparison some obvious parallels have emerged. They are not isolated coincidences but the result of a similar or even identical pattern of thought which includes views on psychology, religion, sin, penance, reform, or any sort of progress. Both men believed implicitly in the workings of Providence and in the futility and downright danger of attempting to alter or even hasten the inscrutable processes of a force superior to human means. When Hawthorne wrote _The Blithedale Romance_, a portrayal of the professional reformer who is neither heroic nor wise but harnessed to an unrealistic theory, his thoughts were like those of Samuel Johnson when he contributed the following four lines to Goldsmith's poem _The Traveller_:

How small of all that human hearts endure,
The part which kings or laws can cause or cure.
Still to ourselves in every place consign'd,
Our own felicity we make or find.

Hawthorne at one time envisioned Brook Farm as a "quest for a better life," but by the time he utilized his utopian experiences in a novel, he wrote:

No sagacious man will long retain his sagacity, if he live exclusively among reformers and progressive people, without periodically returning into the settled system of things. . . .

It was now time for me, therefore, to go and hold a little talk with the conservatives, the writers of the <u>North American Review</u>, the merchants, the politicians, the Cambridge men, and all those respectable old blockheads who still, in this intangibility and mistiness of affairs, kept a death-grip on one or two ideas which had not come into vogue since yesterday morning.[69]

The pattern of conservatism could not be more explicitly defined.

Dr. Johnson's prayers and meditations reveal him to be as much concerned with sin and repentance as the author of <u>The Scarlet Letter</u>. Both these writers were concerned with problems of soul and conscience, sin and redemption. They were both emancipated puritans—men who found that a devoutly spiritual attitude would contribute to, rather than hinder, a man's life among other men. They believed that the only test of truth lay in the validity of human experience, that the traditions derived from human experience must be preserved.

And they were both men who reacted to the social and intellectual issues of their own day. Johnson's England and Hawthorne's America, though nearly a century apart, were experiencing periods of upheaval and innovation. Johnson perceived the effects of experimental science on formal philosophy in the eighteenth century and could not agree with the result; neither could he tolerate the formulation of new attitudes toward man and his environment, attitudes which revised traditional Christian concepts of human nature. In America Hawthorne felt the even greater influence of science and its application to life in the nineteenth century more immediately than could Johnson. He perceived a developing technological force which promised man increased comfort at no human sacrifice, but he was skeptical, and feared the changes being wrought on man and on his environment. He objected also to the tender-minded optimism of his contemporaries who abandoned the restrictions of formal Christianity and found in the individual man an abundance of divinity. In their respective ages then, both Johnson and Hawthorne, though they could not condemn every kind of change, urged their fellow human beings to apply checks to all manner of excess, to any radical scheme which promised

much at little or no cost.   The thought of these two
men runs counter to the popular idea of progress, evident in eighteenth-century England and dominant in
nineteenth-century America.   Like advocates of conservatism today, Johnson and Hawthorne are united not so
much by what they advocated as by what they opposed.

1. Walter J. Bate in his recent study, _The Achievement of Samuel Johnson_ (New York, 1955), 165-7, points out that Johnson's Toryism was a responsible political stance which often ran counter to the _status quo_.

2. Hawthorne subsequently left Brook Farm in disgust; and although he was a Democrat by party designation, he was not a democrat in the sense of advocating social or economic levelling.

3. Percy Hazen Houston, _Doctor Johnson: A Study in Eighteenth Century Humanism_ (Cambridge, Mass., 1923), 7.

4. Russell Kirk, _The Conservative Mind_ (Chicago, 1953), 7-8.

5. _Ibid._, 9.

6. F. O. Matthiessen, _American Renaissance_ (New York, 1941), 206-8. See also Mark Van Doren, _Nathaniel Hawthorne_ (New York, 1949), 32-4.

7. _The Complete Works of Nathaniel Hawthorne_ (Boston, 1891), XI, 175-6.

8. _Ibid._, XII, 298-312.

9. _Ibid._, XVIII, 247.

10. The original passage concerning Johnson's penance at Uttoxetter is to be found in Boswell's _Life of Johnson_ (New York, 1933), I, 501: "Once, indeed, I was disobedient; I refused to attend my father to Uttoxetter Market. Pride was the source of that refusal, and the remembrance of it was painful. A few years ago I desired to atone for this fault; I went to Uttoxetter in very bad weather, and stood for a considerable time bareheaded in the rain, on the spot where my father's stall used to stand." This incident never failed to excite Hawthorne.

11. Hawthorne, _Works_, XI, 176-7.

12. _Loc. cit._

13. _Ibid._, XXI, 36-7.

14. See Frank Davidson, "Hawthorne's Use of a Pattern from 'The Rambler,'" MLN, LXIII (October-December 1948), for more specific citation of Hawthorne's borrowing from Johnson.

15. Hawthorne, _Works_, XVI, 2.

16. Arlin Turner, ed., _Hawthorne as Editor_ (University, La., 1941), 198-9.

17. In "The Threefold Destiny," _Works_, II, 329, Hawthorne begins a tale, which, like _Rasselas_, is concerned with a search for happiness, by stating that he has tried to combine "New England personages and scenery" with "a fairy legend" but hopes that he has not entirely obliterated the sober hues of nature. "Rather than a story of events claiming to be real, it may be considered as an allegory, such as writers of the last century would have expressed in the shape of an Eastern tale, but to which I have endeavored to give a more life-like warmth than could be infused into those fanciful productions."

18. Boswell, _op. cit._, 294, 339.

19. Richard B. Sewall, "Dr. Johnson, Rousseau, and Reform," _The Age of Johnson: Essays Presented to Chauncey Brewster Tinker_ (New Haven, 1949), 313. Compare this with Hawthorne's statement: "No human effort, on a grand scale, has ever yet resulted according to the purpose of its projectors. The advantages are always incidental ("Chiefly about War Matters," _Works_, XVII, 403).

20. Hawthorne, _Works_, V, 227-8.

21. "The Unpardonable Sin might consist in a want of love and reverence for the Human Soul; in consequence of which, the investigator pried into its dark depths, not with a hope or purpose of making it better, but from a cold philosophical curiosity,--content that it should be wicked in whatever kind or degree, and only desiring to study it out. Would not this, in other words, be the separation of the intellect from

the heart." Randall Stewart, ed., <u>The American Note-</u><u>books</u> (New Haven, 1932), 106.

22. Austin Warren, in his introduction to <u>Nathaniel Hawthorne</u> (New York, 1934), would view Haw-thorne's psychology as equating the heart with the will, making the Christian element in Hawthorne even stronger. See Barriss Mills, "Hawthorne and Puri-tanism," NEQ, XXI (March 1948), 92: "By 'heart' in the quoted passage from 'Earth's Holocaust' he meant some-thing not much different from 'soul.'"

23. J. W. Krutch, <u>Samuel Johnson</u> (New York, 1944), 24.

24. <u>The Complete Works of Samuel Johnson</u>, LLD (London, 1825), V, 256. Italics mine.

25. <u>Ibid.</u>, "The Vanity of Human Wishes," I, 22, vv. 360-3. Bate, 95, comments on these same lines from Johnson's poem in a statement very applicable to Haw-thorne's work: "Growth of 'the healthful mind' con-sists in establishing active links of sympathy and understanding with what is outside. Conversely, the 'treachery of the human heart' is what isolated the individual."

26. <u>Ibid.</u>, VII, 340.

27. <u>Ibid.</u>, 339. The resemblance to T. S. Eliot's diagnosis of the "dissociation of sensibility" is not accidental.

28. Hawthorne, <u>Works</u>, XVIII, 10-11.

29. <u>Ibid.</u>, IV, 304.

30. Johnson, <u>Works</u>, I, 204.

31. <u>Ibid.</u>, 207.

32. <u>Ibid.</u>, 248.

33. <u>Ibid.</u>, 249. The climate of optimistic benevo-lism in the above quotation presumes Shaftesbury's major theses: 1. A belief in the divine perfection of "Nature" (in the sense of the whole order of creation); 2. A natural rather than revealed religion; 3. A belief

in the essential goodness of man; 4. The conviction that virtue is "to follow Nature."

34. Randall Stewart, ed., _The American Notebooks_, 168.

35. Boswell, _op. cit._, I, 501.

36. Hawthorne, _Works_, IV, 260-1.

37. _Ibid._, 275. Italics mine.

38. Hawthorne's distrust of technological innovation in this tale--both the railroad and the steamboat are conveyances of the Fiend--suggests another important area of comparison with Johnson and another facet of the conservative pattern. For the conservative realizes the inefficacy of technological progress in matters crucial to human life. Thus Hawthorne's "Hall of Fantasy," a meeting-place for numerous half-baked theorists, also houses a goodly number of inventors and their machines. And in _Rasselas_, Johnson does not overlook the folly of the inventor who fashions a means for flying. The mechanical wings fail to sustain the inventor, and he appears ridiculous in contrast to Imlac--poet, scholar, and philosopher whose realistic guidance infuses a sense of tragedy to a story which might have been only resigned pessimism. It is Imlac who thus voices Johnson's sentiments on the value of technological invention in securing human happiness. Though Imlac knows that the civilized Europeans have advanced means for curing wounds and diseases, comfortable shelters for escaping the rigors of the weather, powerful "engines for the despatch of many laborious works," and effective "communication between distant places," he says "the Europeans are less unhappy than we, but they are not happy. Human life is every where a state, in which much is to be endured, and little to be enjoyed" (Johnson, _Works_, I, 225-6).

39. Johnson, _Works_, I, 237-8.

40. _Ibid._, 239-41.

41. Hawthorne, _Works_, I, 71.

42. _Ibid._, 72.

43. "It was his labour [said Johnson of Socrates] to turn philosophy from the study of [external] nature to speculations upon life, but the innovators whom I oppose are turning off attention from life to nature. They seem to think, that we are placed here _to watch the growth of plants, or the motion of the stars_. Socrates was rather of opinion, that what we had to learn was, _how to do good, and avoid evil_" (Johnson, _Works_, VII, 77). Italics mine.

44. _Ibid._, I, 288.

45. _Ibid._, 292-4. Italics mine.

46. Hawthorne, _Works_, IV, 49-52.

47. _Ibid._, 52.

48. _Ibid._, 56-7. Italics mine.

49. _Ibid._, 76-7. Italics mine.

50. Johnson, "The Vanity of Human Wishes," _Works_, I, 22, vv. 367-70.

51. _Works_, I, 300. Italics mine.

52. _Ibid._, 301-2. Italics mine.

53. _Ibid._, 302.

54. Hawthorne, _Works_, IV, 124.

55. _Ibid._, I, 59.

56. Johnson, _Works_, I, 264-5.

57. _Ibid._, 222-3.

58. Matthiessen, _op cit._, 320.

59. For these comments on "The Gray Champion" I am indebted primarily to Professor B. B. Cohen.

60. Hawthorne, _Works_, I, 2.

61. _Ibid._, 14. Compare this with Johnson's statement: "And then, Sir, there is this consideration,

that if the abuse be enormous, Nature will rise up, and claiming her original rights, overturn a corrupt political system," Boswell, *op. cit.*, I, 284 (his italics). Both men have Providence or nature, some supernatural force, effect this change, rather than man effecting it himself.   It becomes natural law.

62.   Boswell, *op. cit.*, I, 71.   See also *Rambler* No. 180, *Works*, III, 341-5.

63.   Hawthorne, "Earth's Holocaust," *Works*, V, 219.

64.   Johnson, *Works*, I, 269.

65.   Hawthorne, *Works*, II, 305-6.

66.   Johnson, *Works*, I, 308.

67.   Hawthorne, *Works*, II, 299.

68.   Randall Stewart, ed., *The English Notebooks by Nathaniel Hawthorne* (New York, 1941), 101.

69.   Hawthorne, *The Blithedale Romance*, *Works*, VIII, 200-201.

II

"BARTLEBY," MELVILLE'S CIRCUMSCRIBED SCRIVENER

"Bartleby" is certainly the most familiar of Melville's short stories, reprinted in dozens of anthologies and analyzed by scores of critics. It would be hard to say something new about this early study of alienation, frustration, and catatonic withdrawal, and the surest guard against originality, I suspect, would be to take account of every commentary on the story. It would be more foolish, however, to try to clear one's mind completely of what others have written about Melville's pitiable and peculiar clerk and the initially complacent but ultimately vulnerable lawyer who narrates the tale.[1]

This was Melville's first published short story and constitutes a remarkable attempt at a new genre and a considerable recovery from his disappointment over the public reception of Pierre. It was a greater recovery in terms of technical virtuosity than in the expression of a more positive outlook, especially in regard to the title character, who, we have been frequently told, confronts the dismal prospects of the aspiring American artist or writer. It was a subject which, quite understandably, never ceased to interest, attract, and challenge Melville—whether in the general terms of the nature of art, the strengths and liabilities of the artist, or the particular circumstances of the American scene. One or more phases of this complex issue are present in Typee, Mardi, Redburn, White-Jacket, Moby Dick, Pierre, The Confidence-Man, and at least one-third of the short stories. The height of Melville's faith in what the serious writer could accomplish in America occurred in his enthusiastic review of Hawthorne's Mosses, but he reached the depths in Pierre and the two short works that followed in the early 1850's—"Bartleby" and "Cock-a-Doodle-Doo!"

To approach "Bartleby" only as an analogue of the alienated artist in an insensitive society is to ignore a great deal of the contextual richness or symbolic suggestiveness of the story. The stony impersonality of urban America so prominent in the latter part of Pierre is compressed into the Wall Street law office setting of "Bartleby" and both stories end with the death of the title character in the steel and granite isolation of the Tombs--the would-be writer crushed by the ponderous judgments of a matter-of-fact society. In each case the title character's pathetic end is a compound of his personality (ideals, expectations, delusions, and compulsions) and the pressures of a pragmatic, profit-oriented, and apparently unsympathetic society. And in each case also, the character's psychological demise and ultimate death follows a breakdown in communication between himself and his society.

When "Bartleby" first appeared (in two installments of _Putnam's Monthly_ in late 1853), the title read "Bartleby, the Scrivener. A Story of Wall-Street." The shorter form adopted later was very likely the result of typographical considerations in listing the contents of Melville's _Piazza Tales_, where all the titles are brief; and since the _Piazza Tales_ has been the source of most subsequent republications of the story, the shorter title has become the more familiar. This circumstance is unfortunate because it plays down the social and economic connotations of "Wall-Street" and the degree to which Bartleby was described or identified by his employment in the original title. Melville's intention, it seems likely, was to use the extended title to emphasize the highly dramatic, actually expressionistic, Wall Street setting--a law office where the four employees are literally and figuratively _walled_ in by the circumstances of their employment and by the social assumptions embodied in their employer and _walled off_ from any hope of mobility or self-fulfillment by the same concept of class structure.

In a less obvious sense than in _White-Jacket_, where the United States ship _Neversink_ was a man-of-war representation of an overwhelmingly hierarchical society with distinct class and caste divisions, the Wall Street office is a microcosmic representation of a simpler but similarly structured segment of American society. To Bartleby--who secures employment as a legal copyist, a sort of animated Xerox machine duplicating the documents that reinforce and perpetuate the _status quo_--the office seems a dead-end existence, denying his unique human individuality, curtailing his freedom of choice, and corroborating his hopelessness. His withdrawal from what his employer would judge to be socially productive activity into his "dead-wall revery" is Bartleby's resentful confirmation of the gross inequities and subtle iniquities of an existence that is servile at best and imprisoning at worst. Although he somehow obtains a key to the office, Bartleby chooses to remain permanently within an enclosure with no exit, a prisoner who is also his own jailer, so that when he is imprisoned in the Tombs and surrounded by the massive walls, his condition seems changed hardly at all. To his own satisfaction--or more accurately, dissatisfaction--he has proved that democratic theory masks despotic practice, that the supposedly open society can easily be closed off by those in power, and that Christian principle can be stretched to cover exploitative sham. But Melville grants Bartleby only a measure of truth and more than a modicum of distortion and delusion. He is a character akin to Kafka's Josef K. or Gregor Samsa, but his story is not as simple as one of Kafka's grotesque allegories. Disenchanted as he often was, Melville did not yet view American society as the Amerika of some present-day critics.

Technically "Cock-a-Doodle-Doo!" is a more Kafkaesque story than "Bartleby." For one thing the narrator in the former story becomes more and more subject to his hallucinatory perception of reality; whereas the narrator in "Bartleby" suffers the loss of his comforting preconceptions and brushes against an aspect of reality he could not earlier have imagined. More important perhaps, is the fact that we see nothing from Bartleby's point of view and have to guess at what ails him, both aided and hindered by the narrator's perception of Bartleby's symptoms and his interpretation of Bartleby's actions. As the narrator says in the opening paragraph, "Bartleby was one of those beings of whom nothing is ascertainable, except from the original sources, and, in his case, those are very small" (p. 3).[2] Despite the scarcity of sources, we are given an extensive case history of Bartleby's last days. It is provided entirely by the narrator, who is a very unlikely and somewhat unwilling evangelist. His account thus has its inherent limitations, but it is the only gospel we have and it will have to suffice.

Melville's handling of the point of view in this story is a conscious and sustained artistic achievement, an exercise in irony unprecedented in American literature. Without apparent strain he manipulated his narrator so that this well-heeled, self-satisfied source both reveals and obscures the meaning of his troubling experiences. Not by any means an entirely unreliable narrator, this representative of conservative business interests is a man of realistically limited perception but capable of considerable moral growth. Melville's most telling tactic, much like that of Mark Twain in <u>Huckleberry Finn</u> but more subtle, is to make the narrator's language suggest far more than the character consciously realizes. Thus his attitudes, his actions and reactions, but more importantly his vocabulary, mark the meanings that his mind cannot reach and establish the three dimensions of the story.

To understand those dimensions, we are required to approach them, at least in part, from Bartleby's point of view, to approximate his perspective. The first dimension (or direction of implicative meaning) involves the concept of <u>community</u>--an ideal that is social, political, and economic. The second involves the concept of <u>communication</u>, which extends the social function into areas of literary or artistic implication. And the third involves the concept of <u>communion</u>, the significance of which is obviously spiritual or religious. These dimensions are related and partially overlap while still being distinguishable. Yet from our growing intuition of Bartleby's point of view, each seems to have held forth a glowing possibility only to have it disproved by some impenetrable obstacle-- physical, social, or metaphysical. The various walls, tangibly representing the obstacles Bartleby has found in his experience, inevitably shape his perspective and deny him any further prospect.

In American society, where promise is so great and expectation so high, Bartleby finds no place to go and no fulfillment in life. He lapses into lethargy; flouts the obligations of a work-money-property-oriented society; stubbornly asserts the negative aspects of his freedom of will; and in withdrawing from the world of social affairs and human relationships, seems to will his withdrawal from life itself. There is no clear diagnosis of what Bartleby suffers from, but there is enough evidence to construct a complex pathology, demonstrating that Melville found the sources of this condition in the character of the existing society and in the peculiar susceptibilities of the sensitive individual.

The main dimension of the story is concerned with the idea of _community_, or rather the lack of it, within the physical and social divisions of the Wall Street office. The narrator's estimate of himself and his relationship to his subordinates tells us a great deal. The possessive pronoun is prominent as he tells about "myself, my _employés_, my business, my chambers." Like the complacent lawyers in "The Paradise of Bachelors," men insulated from the troubling trials of life who used the law to right no wrongs, the narrator has sought "the cool tranquility of a snug retreat" where he can "do a snug business among rich men's bonds, and mortgages, and title-deeds." He prides himself for being known as a "safe" man and for possessing such virtues as "prudence" and "method." Morality, justice, sympathy, or passion are outside his value system. He unashamedly loves money and venerates "the late John Jacob Astor," whose name becomes part of the narrator's litany "for it hath a rounded and orbicular sound to it, and rings like unto bullion." Connotatively "Astor" suggests not only wealth but in combination with "orbicular" it also suggests a heavenly sphere in which the financial luminary "Astor" is the source of light and emotive power. And the narrator is not merely a well-to-do American or a spokesman for Wall Street, he is unabashedly an idolater of the golden bull—now become the almighty dollar. His priesthood of profit and his proprietary air shape his attitude toward the men who work for him. "My _employés_" could be a way of speaking, or it could mean that they have value as means to serve my financial ends (pp. 3-4).

This tendency of the narrator to judge others by their utility to him seems to make him more tolerant of human weakness or eccentricity, but in a very damaging way it mocks the possibility of men joining in a common enterprise founded on self-respect and sympathy. He is a benevolent master of his men and an enlightened employer-exploiter. He can put up with Turkey's excessive drinking, irritability, and carelessness if the elderly clerk remains useful and productive for a predictable part of the day. (Since he pays his copyists on a piecework rate rather than a salary, he can be more tolerant of their unproductive periods.) Turkey cannot be relied on in the afternoon but Nippers, the

other copyist, could be counted on to do his best work
then. So between them these two employees (identified
like Ginger Nut, the office boy, only by the demeaning
nicknames which turn them into things) produced a good
day's work--a situation which the narrator accepts as
"a good natural arrangement, under the circumstances"
(p. 10). Their greatest value, their existential purpose, is their service as distinct instrumentalities
and not as individual human beings.

Of the two clerks, Nippers is easily the more
ambitious, impatient at the routine and menial aspects
of his employment and anxious to "be rid of a scrivener's table altogether." But instead of admiring Nippers for his enterprise, the narrator calls it "his
diseased ambition"; instead of praising his attempts to
raise his social position, the narrator charges him
with "a continual discontent" (p. 8). From the employer's point of view, Nippers is too uppity: he ought to
know his place and accept it more graciously. Instead,
he envies and in some small way assumes a few perqui-
sites of power. These traits make him seem to his
employer an insidious and even at times a satanic
threat to system and authority. Yet because Nippers'
eccentricities were evident only when Turkey's were
not, both men remained tolerably useful to their employer.

The narrator's essentially selfish standards and
the superficial values of Wall Street society underlie
his description of his employees' appearances and the
acceptability of their dress. He can, for example,
more easily overlook Nippers' shortcomings because "he
always dressed in a gentlemanly sort of way; and so,
incidentally, reflected credit upon my chambers." Turkey's clothes, however, were more apt to be messy and
ill-fitting, and so the narrator, in an act of self-
serving charity, gave him one of his own more "respect-
able-looking" coats, assuming that Turkey would show
his appreciation by curbing his afternoon rashness.
Instead of being useful and productive and a greater
credit to his employer's establishment, Turkey reacted
resentfully to what his employer cannot recognize as a
demeaning form of charity; and the narrator's explanation further degrades his employee: "too much oats are
bad for horses . . . [and] precisely as a rash, restive
horse is said to feel his oats, so Turkey felt his
coat. It made him insolent. He was a man whom pros-

41

perity harmed" (p. 9). The attitude underlying the narrator's remarks is extremely class (or caste) oriented and Turkey, like Nippers, is guilty of not knowing his place and not responding properly to what his employer has so graciously bestowed on him. The narrator's reasons for hiring Bartleby so quickly, after merely "a few words touching his qualification," have to do largely with his appearance and dress-- "singularly sedate," "pallidly neat, pitiably respectable"--and the hope that he would be a steadying influence on the uneven tempers of Nippers and Turkey, a model of the neatness, servility, dependence, obedience, gratitude, and contentment the master wants in his scriveners.

The narrator's supreme position in this social microcosm is understood by his employees' normally deferential attitudes, prefacing their statements with phrases like "with submission, sir" or "excuse me," very much as verbal communication with a reigning monarch would be prefaced with "by your grace." (In marked contrast, however, is Bartleby's "I prefer not to"--a subtly scaled down or understated "non serviam.") The need for a third clerk is occasioned by the increased business resulting from what the narrator terms "receiving the Master's office" (p. 11). It is a conveniently abbreviated way of referring to his position as a Master in Chancery, but it further stresses the social, economic, and psychological relationship between the narrator and his clerks. The appointment to this office was not only a very lucrative circumstance, as the narrator points out, but it also conveyed considerable quasi-judicial power. A Master in Chancery rendered decisions in those matters of equity which the common law did not cover and the courts were not constituted to settle. There is irony, of course, in the narrator's being responsible for determining matters of equity--what is fair, just, and impartial-- when his Wall Street ways are so fraught with inequities. And there is further irony in the legal definition of _equity_ which would apply the dictates of conscience or principles of natural justice to settle controversies. Needless to say, the partiality and self-interest of the narrator are never in doubt and his conscience is merely the internalized dictates of Wall Street. Melville may have had still more in mind in calling such considerable attention to "the Master's office," for _chancery_ can refer to "a wrestling hold that imprisons the head or encircles the neck," and in legal usage the phrase _in chancery_ can mean "in a helpless, hopeless, or embarrassing position." It would not have been beyond Melville to use such legalistic and lexicographical puns to stress the subjugation of Wall Street's white-collar proletariat. He could be even more blatant on this score in his indictment of socially respectable white slavery in "The Tartarus of Maids."

The divisions and confinements that underlie the social relationships are more tangibly embodied in the physical arrangements of the office. It becomes "a house divided" because such an arrangement fulfills the narrator's conception of propriety, proprietorship, and utility. It easily could be the stage setting for a work of twentieth-century expressionism:

> Ground-glass folding-doors divided my premises into two parts, one of which was occupied by my scriveners, the other by myself. According to my humor, I threw open these doors, or closed them. I resolved to assign Bartleby a corner by the folding doors, but on my side of them so as to have this quiet man within easy call, in case any trifling thing was to be done. I placed his desk close up to a small side-window. . . . Within three feet of the panes was a wall, and light came down from far above, between two lofty buildings, as from a very small opening in a dome. Still further to a satisfactory arrangement, I procured a high green folding screen, which might entirely isolate Bartleby from my sight, though not remove him from my voice. And thus, in a manner, privacy and society were conjoined (pp. 11-12).

In these circumstances Bartleby, at least initially, "did an extraordinary quantity of writing," copying through the night as well as day. But it was writing done on command, with as much originality as a machine could muster. When the narrator wants Bartleby to aid in proofreading, he calls with the "natural expectancy of instant compliance," and instead of compliance, Bartleby issues his first "I would prefer not to" (p. 13). The narrator sits stunned and unbelieving, as Bartleby's assertion of autonomy throws into turmoil the carefully controlled network of assumptions, expectations, and relationships.

43

In his quiet way Bartleby terrorizes the Wall Street establishment. His understated parody of Satan's refusal implies a greater threat than Nippers' acts of resentment, but only in the dubious light of the Wall Street establishment, which he will not serve, does Bartleby appear a satanic character. From a different perspective there might be a noble madness in the stubborn obstructiveness and passive withdrawal which constitute the developing strategy of his peculiar and paradoxical insurrection.

In one sense it is merely that Bartleby knows his place and will not leave it; in another sense his immobilized behavior seems an act of gross contempt for the conventions of a property-and-profit-oriented society. His appropriation of private property for personal use—first sleeping in the office and then staging a passive sit-in when directed to leave—strikes at the heart of the system. It also hits the narrator where he lives, as it were: he first feels "disarmed" by Bartleby's quiet rebellion and ultimately feels "unmanned" by the threat to his authority (pp. 14, 21).

However weakened he personally feels, the narrator finds his role forced on him and his will stiffened by the Wall Street society that has served him so well. He must now serve that society and not Bartleby's crippling eccentricity. By the standards of that society Bartleby is a perverse nut, and for the narrator to continue to tolerate him would be sheer insanity. He is caught between the attitude of blandly benign accommodation, which has enabled him to turn so many circumstances to his own benefit, and the social rigidities and conformist practices of Wall Street, which will permit no such perversity or eccentricity as Bartleby's. His decision to oust Bartleby reflects the pressure of the business community which determines substantially his status and identity, and his rather bland, apologetic explanation is that "necessities connected with my business tyrannized over all other considerations" (p. 29). On Wall Street, apparently, good form, conformity, and business forms are the essential means of communication; thus the narrator's hoped for farewell to Bartleby (after giving him an amount in excess of wages due) concludes with phraseology taken directly from the form of business correspondence: "If, hereafter, in your new place of abode, I can be of any service to you, do not fail to advise me by letter" (p. 30). The message and the gift preceding it are a form of literal generosity but clearly lacking the spirit of genuine charity, and in their formality both gift and message discourage further communication and deny any idea of community.

When Bartleby fails to leave the premises as he has been directed, the narrator, with unconscious irony, puts the matter on a basis of business law, asking first, "What earthly right have you to stay here?"--not realizing that something more than "earthly right" might be involved. Then he follows with questions that again stress the profit-property nexus of Wall Street and of the culture at large: "Do you pay any rent? Do you pay my taxes? Or is this property yours" (p. 33). Bartleby remains silent; these are not his questions, and his seemingly contemptuous withdrawal infuriates the narrator. In trying prudently to check his anger, he begins to recognize the lack of communal attachments in circumstances like those of his office. He recalls a recent murder case that must have been of note to the New York business community and wonders whether "the circumstance of being alone in a solitary office, upstairs, of a building entirely unhallowed by humanizing domestic associations" did not help trigger the act (p. 34).

His innate prudence makes him seek an alternative to anger toward Bartleby, one that will soothe his sensibilities without offending his practical businessman's principles. His first refuge is a form of prudential charity but predicated on self-interest. His second is a kind of pragmatic predestination that glosses his providential relationship to Bartleby. But neither of these theological or philosophical rationalizations enables him to withstand the continuing pressure from his professional peers, and his conscience--more properly his malleable conscientiousness--caves in. Yet thrust Bartleby into the street, he cannot; so he takes the unlikely course of moving his offices to another location, leaving Bartleby behind, breaking any possible connection, denying any further responsibility.

While Melville, through artfully constructed narrative, conveys a strong sense of the obstacles to community and the barriers to communication, he also drops hints of further enclosure, separation, or divi-

45

sion. For one thing the narrator's description of his
own power and authority melds into a supremacy that is
more than social or economic. In describing Turkey's
daily rhythm, he praises him for being "the blandest
and most _reverential_ of men in the morning," especially, "valuing his morning _services_" and resenting "his
afternoon _devotions_" (when he is rash and excessively
spirited). This deference and reverence is, of course,
directed toward the narrator, who refers to himself as
"a _man of peace_" (pp. 6-7). These italicized terms
might be merely a mildly humorous sort of irony were it
not for the kind of vocabulary used in reference to
Bartleby, or as a consequence of Bartleby. His first
appearance is referred to as his "advent" (p. 5). He
is "this forlornest of mankind" (p. 26); and for the
puzzled and troubled narrator, he is "not only useless
as a necklace, but afflictive to bear" (p. 29). Several apparently unconscious puns on the word "assumption"
spin off the narrator's reaction to Bartleby (pp. 31-
32), and the narrator also speaks of Bartleby's "cadaverous triumph" and his "ascendency" (pp. 32-33). Such
a "string" of linked multiple meanings cannot be accidental, and most readers will recognize that these
terms have special application in Christian worship.

Moreover, Bartleby is described repeatedly in
terms that stress his lack of coloration, his silence,
his omnipresence, and his seeming perpetuity—all of
which give him a supernatural cast. He is "pallidly
neat" upon his first appearance, and later the narrator
is "awed into . . . tame compliance" by Bartleby's
"pallid haughtiness" (pp. 11, 24). All told, the words
pallid, pale, pallor, or some similar variation are
used fifteen times and _white_ and _gray_ once each in
reference to Bartleby. Words that stress his silence—
quiet, calm, mute, still, noiseless, as well as _silent_
and other synonyms—appear more than twenty times. The
emphasis on these attributes is important because of
Melville's tendency to associate them with larger-than-
life, awe-inspiring forces. To the narrator Bartleby
also appears variously as an "apparition," "strange
creature," "incubus," "ghost," or "haunt." Unlike
other men, he never reads, never drinks beer, tea, or
coffee, and seems to eat rarely and then only the
spiced wafers called ginger nuts. In what seems an
ironic commentary on the sacrament of communion,
Bartleby dines on these wafers in solitude. Mystery
surrounds his past; and his silence regarding his ori-

gins, family, motives, or complaints--Bartleby's own refusal to communicate--pushes the mystery into the present.

But before concluding that Bartleby is Christ (as Bruce Franklin, drawing heavily from the explication of Christian charity in Matthew 25, has done), I would like to suggest that Melville has left room for a natural explanation as well as a supernatural one. Bartleby's symptoms could substantiate a diagnosis of severe mental illness; that is, his condition could be that of a man who is suffering from the delusion that he is Christ and reacting to the indifference, self-absorption, or ridicule of mid-nineteenth-century American society. Or even without the presence of such a delusion, Bartleby's condition could be the consequence of a sensitive individual's reaction to the insensitivity of his surroundings, and a present-day psychoanalyst would find the symptoms forming a familiar composite.

In the taxonomy of schizophrenia provided by one contemporary psychiatrist, for example, we find the following symptoms for the type of catatonia which is characterized by stupor, with "an apparent, but not real, diminution of consciousness":

i. Negativism, echolalia
ii. Automatism, dreaminess, grimacing
iii. Immobility, waxy flexibility
iv. Refusal to eat[3]

Bartleby's negativism permeates every phase of his behavior, but it can be viewed as a distorted form of autonomy, an attempt at affirming the "I," a passive protest at depersonalization. And his repeated response "I prefer not to" differs from the typical echolalia, in which the affected individual repeats the interviewer's or therapist's statements. Bartleby echoes and thereby asserts only himself. Automatism, of course, characterized his action before and after his refusal to work. First he worked day and night, copying "silently, palely, mechanically," then withdrew behind his screen into the dreamy, immobile state that the narrator terms "his dead-wall revery" (pp. 12, 28). The narrator compares Bartleby to a "pale plaster-of-paris bust of Cicero" (p. 13). Dr. Rosenbaum, describing schizophrenic patients in a catatonic stupor, writes that they "adopt strange, uncomfortable-looking, statuelike postures which they maintain for minutes or hours at a time" (p. 26). The narrator supposes that Bartleby's immobility and refusal to work are due to eye strain, "for his eyes looked dull and glazed" (p. 28). Rosenbaum explains that in this catatonic condition patients' "faces may portray dreaminess, grimacing, or tics, and frequently one has the impression that they are locked into contact with hallucinations to which . . . they cannot respond" (p. 28). The narrator is depressed by the thought of Bartleby's meager diet and after his removal to the tombs tries to provide more amply, but Bartleby refuses to eat and dies "huddled" and "wasted" on the stones "at the base of the wall" (p. 45). Dr. Rosenbaum concludes his description, observing that "such patients may frequently be so immobilized that they neither eat nor maintain sphincter control" and adding that "tube feedings may be necessary to avoid death through inanition" (p. 27). The symptomatology is remarkably similar in these instances, and the similarity is probably more than a matter of coincidence. Perhaps Melville offered a serious diagnosis when he had the twelve-year-old office boy in the story say of Bartleby, "I think, sir, he's a little _luny_" (p. 16, Melville's italics).[4]

But Melville's story is much more than a case history, and my purpose is not to force such a conjectural psychoanalysis of a fictional figure whose author, many will hasten to say, antedated the concepts and classifications of contemporary psychoanalysis. (There are too many instances when Melville's imagination led him to treat symbolically what social or behavioral science had not yet articulated for anyone to be long troubled by the thought that Melville could not have known such things. The serious artist is often surrogate psychoanalyst and vicarious victim in one.) My purpose here is to propose that Melville could have meant the natural explanation and the supernatural suggestions of Bartleby's behavior to reinforce each other in a more complex way than his friend Hawthorne had done in offering natural and supernatural alternatives.

To put it most simply, Bartleby is incapacitated by having internalized the schism that frustrates authentic community, intellectual and emotional communication, and spiritual communion. He has become a divided self, a kind of symbolic embodiment of what ails man and society. Obsessed by the imperfection around him, he is also affronted by such inadequate measures to make things right as having to verify copy. There is far more that cannot be made right in the human relationships that exist, in the lack of recognition or reinforcement for individual members of this false community on Wall Street. Having concluded, apparently, that in the kind of existence where vital reinforcement is unavailable, frustration is inevitable, Bartleby has no faith in what might possibly sustain him and opts out.

In requiring the reader to approximate Bartleby's vantage point even as the events are recounted by his establishment-oriented employer, Melville has anticipated the sort of challenge that R. D. Laing has issued to traditional psychoanalysis. His approach is not to classify psychotic patients as examples of disease but, by approximating the point of view of the patient in his particular environmental circumstances, to show how apparently odd or irrelevant behavior can be meaningful and appropriate. Schizophrenia thus appears a psychological strategy devised to defend the victim's humanity in the midst of threatening circumstances, and even his most bizarre behavior can be seen as a comprehensible response to his immediate situation. The parallel to Melville's story is quite remarkable as Laing seeks to anchor the explanation of psychotic symptoms in the social setting of the patient. (See the "Preface to the Pelican Edition" of The Divided Self, p. 11.)

Ironically, Bartleby has had an effect and both minor and major changes are in process. Nippers and Turkey, as well as the narrator, come to use the word "prefer" with increasing frequency (while unaware that they use it at all) and thereby show the subtle impact of Bartleby, who also remains unaware of his power to make involuntary converts even among those who oppose him or make him the target of their separate hostilities. He also seems unaware that an important personality change is in process in his employer whose efforts at charity, at first so prudential and pragmatic, become increasingly suffused with a sense of humanity and compassion. Although he never completely breaks free from his Wall Street proprieties, he shows less need to rationalize his actions or find a utilitarian justification for them. His private reflections reveal not only the growth of tolerance and sympathy,

49

but also the greater profundity of a spiritual conversion:

> For the first time in my life a feeling of overpowering stinging melancholy seized me. Before, I had never experienced aught but a not unpleasing sadness. The bond of a common humanity now drew me irresistibly to gloom. A fraternal melancholy! For both I and Bartleby were sons of Adam. I remembered the bright silks and sparkling faces I had seen that day . . . and I contrasted them with the pallid copyist, and thought to myself, Ah, happiness courts the light, so we deem that misery there is none. These sad fancyings . . . led on to other and more special thoughts, concerning the eccentricities of Bartleby. Presentiments of strange discoveries hovered around me. The scrivener's pale form appeared to me laid out, among uncaring strangers, in its shivering winding-sheet (p. 23).

"The bond of a common humanity," upon which the ideal of community and the concept of communion both depend, is not constant in the narrator's consciousness. The pressure of his Wall Street peers is still there, affecting him both before and after his move to new quarters. The new tenant who finds Bartleby is no more successful in getting him to work or to leave and when he seeks out the narrator to question him about his former employee, the narrator admits to no personal knowledge of or responsibility for Bartleby. In fact he denies Bartleby three times publicly before returning to his old quarters in a final effort to oust him. Bartleby, however, shows no interest in any other possible employment and refuses the narrator's remarkably generous offer to take him into his own home.

He has seen something more in the offer than generosity and his refusal indicates his unwillingness to expose himself further to the kind of situation that has repeatedly victimized him. The situation has all the characteristics of what Gregory Bateson and his associates first formulated as the "double-bind." In Self and Others, Laing summarizes the concept and offers his view of its sequential ingredients: 1) two or more persons, one of whom can be designated the "victim"; 2) a repeated pattern that comes to be a habitual expectation in the victim's experience; 3) a negative

50

injunction, such as the narrator's "if you do not go away from these premises . . . , I shall feel bound--indeed, I _am_ bound . . . ," followed by a threat of abandonment (p. 41); 4) a secondary injunction conflicting with the first communicated by either verbal or nonverbal means, and absolving the narrator from responsibility for whatever punishment follows, as in the narrator's offer to take Bartleby into his home with the unspoken injunction that Bartleby will subsequently have to do his part; and 5) a further injunction prohibiting the victim from escaping, sealing him into the situation, as the symbolic walls or the narrator's reacting to Bartleby's immobility with "stationary you shall be, then," seem to have done. Once an individual has come to perceive his relationship in double-bind patterns, almost any part of the expected sequence can be enough to precipitate the end result. For Bartleby, who has learned to expect this kind of entrapment, any attempt at communication invites catastrophe, existence becomes increasingly circumscribed, the walls more rigid, permanent, and inescapable.

In a scene that must be an ironic reversal of Christ driving the money-men from the Temple, Wall Street landlords and city authorities with considerable difficulty remove Bartleby from the Wall Street office, arrest him as a vagrant, and lock him in the Tombs. When the narrator visits him there, he can stimulate in Bartleby no will to live, and Bartleby's last words to the narrator, who has tried to indicate what encouragement exists even in this environment, are, appropriately enough, "I know where I am," and indeed this place of total enclosure is not unfamiliar--the same encircling walls, the same repressive and punitive normality, and the same stony embodiment of antihuman institutions. The narrator imagines Bartleby spending his last days amid "murderers and thieves," tries unsuccessfully to provide him with food, and describes him, after he has died, as asleep "with kings and counselors" (p. 46). The phraseology is extraordinarily portentous, yet somehow appropriate to "this forlornest of mankind."

Appended to the story is an unconfirmed rumor about Bartleby's previous employment as "a subordinate clerk in the Dead Letter Office at Washington" (p. 46). Its position compels us to consider the paragraph even more carefully than the narrator does for its relevance to the preceding account. He sees it as a possible seed bed for Bartleby's negativism and a more certain source of his depression:

> Dead letters! does it not sound like dead men? Conceive a man by nature and misfortune prone to a pallid hopelessness, can any business seem more fitted to heighten it than that of continually handling these dead letters, and assorting them for the flames?

His question is not merely rhetorical, and to some extent he answers it himself. But the question is also a challenge to the reader who has been led through an account of Bartleby's last days in a somewhat stultifying law office in the heart of New York's financial district, where he labored in the service of a man who did "a snug business among rich men's bonds, and mortgages, and title-deeds." Thus part of the answer points to a society where the business of life is business and not life, and to the example of a man who chose the quietest alternative to such a desperate business.

The narrator's answer points to something else, too. Considering those undeliverable letters, he continues:

> For by the cart-load they are annually burned. Sometimes from out the folded paper the pale clerk takes a ring—the finger it was meant for, perhaps, moulders in the grave; a bank-note sent in swiftest charity—he whom it would relieve, nor eats nor hungers any more; pardon for those who died despairing; home for those who died unhoping; good tidings for those who died stifled by unrelieved calamities. On errands of life, these letters speed to death.

> Ah, Bartleby! Ah, humanity! (pp. 46-47)

Undeniably, the narrator's words tend toward the sentimental and the melodramatic, but they are not banal. He has come a long way and has been drawn into a human problem for which there is no neat legal solution. In the only terms he could employ to express his tragic insight, he has called our attention again to the major areas of concern in the story—the frustration of timely communication, the distances between or the barriers to productive human union, the utter despair of those who die still looking for answers, and the essential inhumanity of a society that treats these poignant records of human experience as so much waste for the incinerator. From his earlier perspective he could insist that while there is life there is hope, a way out of any disturbing situation; the sad, concluding sentences of the story offer another view of the human condition: where there is life there is death, the most totally binding and inescapable aspect of existence.

The narrator had begun as a strong proponent of his own ethic of personal enrichment, a gospel of wealth for its own sake, and unexpectedly confronted a mysterious individual who, in an actual or in an ironic sense, represented "the truth that would make men free" and who died in prison himself. But instead of merely re-creating a basic pattern of Christian faith, Melville gives it compelling contemporary relevance by implying that the money-worshiper's utilitarian and demeaning view of men as commodity or chattel is "deicidal" because it is essentially "homicidal." It had cost Nippers and Turkey their full manhood, even before the "advent" of Bartleby. But paradoxically the lawyer-employer-master, who had been instrumental in stifling the human spirit and thereby denying God, is himself a slave to his Wall Street preconceptions. He seems to realize this at the end, but we do not know whether his insight will make him free. Like Emerson in his "Divinity School Address," Melville seems to be saying that any man can be his own Christ, not, however, in the role of serving as his own savior as Emerson insisted, but rather of realizing his own torment, abandonment, and martyrdom.

Despite the religious imagery in the story, there is little sense that death is Bartleby's liberation, somewhat more reason, perhaps, to believe in the narrator's redemption. He has had to serve as a not very willing or successful therapist in a relationship where the victim views his treatment as further persecution and where the narrator-therapist is forced to recognize in the victim an extreme example of what all men are heir to. Having lived as if he were already a prisoner, Bartleby precipitated a sort of self-fulfilling prophecy. Dying in the Halls of Justice, he confirms the metaphors by which he had lived--that the condition of life in human society is as circumscribed as that in a prison, and that a stony refusal is the more telling strategy against surrounding insensitivity.

R. D. Laing has used the term "petrification" to describe the kind of defensive network Bartleby employs. He suggests that an individual who dreads the possibility of being turned into an inanimate object, a machine, or an automaton, and deprived of personal autonomy, may fight back by negating the other person's autonomy, ignoring his feelings, and thereby depersonalizing him--as Bartleby does repeatedly, the last time being his answer to the narrator who has come to the Tombs, seen him, and called his name. Without turning around, Bartleby says, "I know you . . . and I want nothing to say to you" (p. 43). According to Laing, such a contemptuous effort to turn the other person into a thing is a strategy of "nullifying any danger to himself by secretly totally disarming the enemy." Hence there is deep psychological trauma as well as social and economic threat in the circumstances which impel the narrator to refer to himself twice as "disarmed" and twice more as "unmanned." And those circumstances, beginning with Bartleby's first stony refusal, illustrate Laing's reciprocal dynamic of "petrification." The narrator describes his initial reaction in terms of stony transformation: "I was turned into a pillar of salt, standing at the head of my seated column of clerks," but he simultaneously reveals his own earlier depersonalization of his clerks (p. 14). Melville actually seems to have been using this imagery of petrification consciously, for not only is Bartleby early compared to a piece of statuary, he seems, when the narrator gives him money and orders him to leave, "like the last column of some ruined temple" (p. 30). Laing's view, borne out by Melville's story, is that the petrification process "involves a vicious circle. The more one attempts to preserve one's autonomy and identity by nullifying the specific human individuality of the other, the more it is felt to be necessary to continue to do so, because with each denial of the other person's ontological status, one's own ontological security is decreased, the threat to the self from the other is potentiated and hence has to be even more desperately negated" (The Divided Self, p. 52).

54

Bartleby's stony behavior thus could be viewed as an attempt to forestall the threat of being turned into an inanimate thing by his employer, a defensive strategy to avoid being sucked into or engulfed by the narrator's Wall Street whirlpool. To prevent his becoming an object and drawn into his employer's world, Bartleby turns himself into a stubborn and steadfast stone. His function is far more limited than before; he is either an opaque immobility that puzzles and offends his employer or a reflector turning back the other's gaze. Frustrated by the fraudulent communication he has had to participate in, he becomes a silence or an echo--the only communication one gets from a stone.

The narrator's last words express in part his realization of what Bartleby has exemplified and the general susceptibility of humanity to such a view. Not only has Bartleby been physically and psychologically crippled by the pattern of double-binds in his life, but the narrator has recognized his own involvement in the pattern, initially as master and ultimately as victim. Like the therapist who may be drawn into the psychosis of his patient or the lawyer who may participate vicariously in the criminality of his client, the narrator also recognizes that he has furthered the frequently unfair laws of the dominant society. In this sense of a shared fate he has become Bartleby's double, and his account might even be suggesting the universal applicability of such an appalling conclusion. At least he has grasped the general lesson that Bartleby never fully articulated, but we don't know whether he will act on any of its more immediate corollaries, such as the somber irony that there is as much justice in the Tombs as there is equity in the Wall Street law office.

There is no hint of a physical resurrection in the story; Bartleby does not rise from the Tombs, even though some tufts of new grass grow underfoot. But there is a possibility that the narrator has accomplished in his record of mind, memory, and conscience the only immortality Bartleby was to have. Or to put it differently, Melville, in the artfully recreated conscience of his narrator, has ambiguously reaffirmed Bartleby's "cadaverous triumph" and his ultimate "ascendency." And in this sense the narrator's lament for Bartleby and for humanity is prompted by his recognition that for the greater number of persons now alive or yet to be born Bartleby can appear only an unredeemable fool, his contempt for the world an unholy madness, his attempt at social insurrection an abortive failure, and his resurrection out of the question. In Melville's dimly lit theater of hope, life is too often a surrealistic allegory; and art, which could reverse the conventional view of the world and invert the more typical judgments of society, is our feeble means of redemption.

ENDNOTES

1. Among the numerous commentaries on "Bartleby," I would call attention to two in particular for their skill and thoroughness, and for their relevance to the discussion which follows. They are Leo Marx, "Melville's Parable of the Walls," <u>Sewanee Review</u>, Fall, 1953, pp. 602-27 (especially valuable for its discussion of Bartleby's condition as Melville's pessimistic view of the fate of the writer in America and an index to his own state of mind); and H. Bruce Franklin, <u>The Wake of the Gods</u> (Stanford, 1963), pp. 126-36 (memorable for its convincing argument that Bartleby's ascetic withdrawal recapitulates a strain of Hindu mysticism and much of the significance of Christ, in ethical contrast to the way of Wall Street).

2. All page references to "Bartleby" are keyed to Jay Leyda's edition of <u>The Complete Stories of Herman Melville</u> (New York, 1949).

3. C. Peter Rosenbaum, <u>The Meaning of Madness: Symptomatology, Sociology, Biology, and Therapy of the Schizophrenias</u> (New York, 1970), p. 23.

4. The psychodynamics of Bartleby's situation could be better interpreted through some recent post-Freudian developments which stress interpersonal relationships and other factors in the social environment as the cause of personal disturbance, in contradistinction to classical psychoanalysis, which would relate the individual's internal conflict to early experience with parental figures. (Melville's narrator makes a point of saying that no such information about Bartleby's origins or early life is available.)

Recent developments in psychoanalytic thought most relevant to a case like Bartleby's include Harry Stack Sullivan's emphasis on the interpersonal situation, R. D. Laing's view of schizophrenia as an attempt to adjust to an apparently irrational or threatening environment, and, perhaps most important of all, Gregory Bateson's description of dysfunctional modes of communication that convey paradoxical injunctions and result in personal strategies of response clinically identified as schizophrenia.

III

"BENITO CERENO": OLD WORLD EXPERIENCE,
NEW WORLD EXPECTATIONS, AND THIRD WORLD REALITIES

"Benito Cereno" is a story whose time has come.
By that I mean that the concepts essential to understanding the story are now more prevalent than ever
before in American society, assuring the existence of a
sizable, potentially receptive audience. Even so, I
suspect that the guidance offered in the innumerable
college classrooms where students first encounter this
much-anthologized story is as varied as the views expressed in the five decades of "Benito Cereno" criticism. But the story itself is too important a work of
art and an account of cultural confrontation for one to
be detoured into a detailed discussion of the criticism, illuminating as much of it is, misguided as some
of it turns out to be.[1]

Yet the story is itself the chief cause of such
critical variance; the values and preconceptions of
critics are only contributing causes. There is some
basis for charges of murkiness or structural incoher-
ence, but I suspect that Melville's "failure" to
clarify stems more from insight than from oversight.
The story is a remarkable study in the problems of
perception--a subject for which Melville schooled himself in his reading of Shakespeare and Hawthorne, both
of whom, he asserted, were largely misunderstood by
their audiences. In this sense "Benito Cereno" has its
deep source in _Lear_ or _Othello_ rather than Amasa
Delano's _A Narrative of Voyages and Travels, in the
Northern and Southern Hemispheres_ (1817). The immediate source obscured almost as much as it revealed, and
Melville's exploration of individual consciousness and
cultural differences raises problems that Delano never
recognized.

But Delano's _Narrative_ does have an apparent clarity and focus that "Benito Cereno" does not, and the
reader who dislikes the lack of certainty in Melville's
story might actually prefer the more assured, less
ambiguous style of the original. For Melville quite
literally makes his reader the victim of the perceptual
and conceptual difficulties that beset his protagonists, challenging that reader either to abide within

the conceptual worlds of the representatives of American and of Spanish culture or to join him in trying to discern the "truth that comes in with darkness," which neither Delano nor Cereno are capable of penetrating. Like the many-ended intricacies of the Spanish sailor's knot that totally confounds Captain Delano, Melville knots character, setting, symbol, and incident into a cultural puzzle, defying solution. When questioned about the purpose of the knot, the old sailor answered, "For someone else to undo" (296).[2] The answer sums up Melville's challenge to readers of "Benito Cereno" and his awareness that most would drop the knot as meaningless, some would solve it by cutting, and only a few would really struggle to unravel the intricacies.

Critics have long recognized that Amasa Delano embodies prominent New World, specifically North American, attitudes and that Benito Cereno represents a waning Old World culture. But only gradually did there appear any realization that Babo, leader of the rebellious slaves, is a militant spokesman for what are now called, however imprecisely at times, Third World views--here referring to the condition of implicit inferiority that comes of being non-American, non-European, and non-white.

For the greatest part of its length, the third-person narrative is limited and controlled by the consciousness--the values, preconceptions, and outlook--of Amasa Delano, a generous, tolerant, assuredly practical man; in Melville's story he is even a more competent ship's captain than in his own memoir, where he mentions problems of morale and discipline on his own ship and occasionally lapses into a tone of self-pity. While Melville tells his audience that Delano is "a person of a singularly undistrustful good-nature, not liable . . . to indulge in personal alarms, any way involving the imputation of malign evil in man," he also tries to alert a segment of his audience with a line of awkwardly ironic exposition thrown away on most readers: "Whether in view of what humanity is capable, such a trait implies, along with a benevolent heart, more than ordinary quickness and accuracy of perception, may be left to the wise to determine" (256).

That such wise readers existed in significant numbers to support the kind of writer Melville tried to be in the 1850's, he had good reason to doubt. Writing about Melville's relationship to the Harpers, "a firm which had religious connections with Methodism," the late William Charvat described "the problem faced by many American writers of that time—a reading audience so mixed that it was difficult to predict public reactions to deviations from common beliefs and accepted standards of decorum." Charvat went on to say that Melville never was able to assume an audience grouping with "definable degrees of tolerance and sophistication," because the stratification which gives writers a degree of freedom in our time did not begin in America until well after 1850.[3] Yet "Benito Cereno," more than any other of Melville's stories, requires a reader willing to reread the story, ready to reexamine the circumstances, and able to rethink their meaning—a reader who can abandon the comfort of his social assumptions, discern differing points of view, and liberate himself from the confines of conventional expectations and conclusions.

Even with that segment of recent or current readers who catch the cue concerning accuracy of perception, its significance has been perceived differently; and numerous readers whose critical reputations, enlightened social attitudes, and political liberalism are unquestionably solid (F. O. Matthiessen, one case in point) have faulted Melville for his ascription of evil to Babo and the blacks and alleged his underlying insensitivity to the injustice of slavery. They have reacted to the story as if it were a unilateral denunciation of Black Power by Benito Cereno, its pitiable victim, instead of a complex illustration of that "great power of blackness" which Melville discerned in the works of Shakespeare and Hawthorne and which most readers missed or misunderstood, "for it is, mostly insinuated to those who may best understand it, and account for it; it is not obtruded upon every one alike."[4] That "power of blackness" referred not only to the presence of evil in the world and its universal permeation of human personality in a Calvinistic sense; it also presumed gross imperfection in human societies and institutions, a widespread inability of participants to perceive inequity or iniquity, and their ingrained hostility to anyone who presumed to point out so unpopular a truth.

"Let any clergyman try to preach the Truth from its very stronghold, the pulpit, and they would ride

him out of his church on his own pulpit bannister,"
Melville complained to Hawthorne in the famous "Dollars
damn me" letter of June 1851, and further appraising
his potential audience, he added, "What I feel most
moved to write, that is banned. . . . Yet, altogether,
write the other way I cannot." Aware that mid-
nineteenth century Americans, especially successful
ones like the narrator in "Bartleby" or Amasa Delano
himself, had a disproportionately high opinion of themselves, Melville was drawn to expose arrogance and its
demeaning or even dehumanizing effect on human rela-
tionships--not a subject that would endear him to
editors or a sizable part of the reading public. So in
a sense the truth about the well-intentioned white
liberal Protestant American had to be smuggled in
beneath the ban, concealed in the account of the consequences of a slave rebellion at sea. Sensing the
potential explosiveness of this truth, Melville contrived a technique of muffling the detonation or
setting his charges so that the implosion minimized the
shock and hardly made waves.

Also smuggled in covertly is an image of a Negro
leader, unprecedented in American literature. Exploiting the stereotyped behavior familiar to an American
audience, Babo plays two roles simultaneously, while
his true character goes unremarked by the other protagonists, whose "accuracy of perception" is effectively
blocked by those stereotypes. From Amasa Delano's
standpoint Babo is a simple, devoted, sub-human servant, who clearly knows his place; like a dog he is
capable of returning love and loyalty even to a capricious, hard-hearted master. Fulfilling Delano's expectations, Babo projects an image of fidelity that easily
wins the American's admiration and confidence. To
Benito Cereno, however, he seems a heartless savage, an
amoral monster inspired by pure evil. It was not until
the 1950's that there appeared among some few members
of Melville's most appreciative readership the beginnings of a new estimate of Babo; not until the acceler-
ation of the civil rights movement, the rise of black
consciousness, and the published works of Malcolm X,
Franz Fanon, and Eldridge Cleaver were white readers of
"Benito Cereno" prepared to approximate the standpoint
of Babo, discuss his motivation, and appreciate his
intelligence and ingenuity. But even during the 1950's
some have felt that Melville made changes in Amasa
Delano's memoir intended to blacken the blacks and

whiten the whites and that he deserves censure for pushing a pro-slavery position to cash in on a ready market by capitalizing on anti-Negro fears and feelings. (Careful reading hardly supports such a view. Furthermore, the newly appointed editor of Putnam's in 1855 was Frederick Law Olmstead, whose anti-slavery views strongly influenced editorial policy. Putnam's published both "The Bell-Tower" and "Benito Cereno" during the year of Olmstead's editorship.) Even now there are readers, black as well as white, who see an attempt to get Melville off the hook of racism in the suggestion that Babo is an underground hero because of his creative use of symbols to further the blacks' quest for freedom, his remarkable performance as actor-director of the theatrical deception, and his refusal to yield to the combined force of Old and New World law and religion.

Audience receptiveness toward the character of a militant, black artist-activist, directing the slumbering forces in that area of black concentration which Melville was perhaps the first to label "the ghetto," must have been low in mid-nineteenth-century America. Readers in the 1970's are better able to recognize the crippling deficiencies of Delano and Cereno and see Babo as the most fully developed example of manhood in the story, which itself becomes a kind of underground revenge tragedy of a bad dude who was offed because he too successfully had directed artful cunning and purposeful violence at Old and New World oppressors. As the legal deposition makes clear, though Babo himself never articulates it, there is a Cleaver-like logic behind his decision to kill Alexandro Aranda after the mutiny. The murder, preparation of the skeleton, and its use as replacement for the figurehead of Christopher Columbus--whose name and deeds signify the Old World's religious, political, and cultural imperialism--this murder and its horrifying, symbolic warning to the surviving whites that they too may follow their leader, temporal or spiritual, is itself a political act, fully rational and justifiable from Babo's standpoint. For as long as Aranda lived, they could not be legally free; in the eyes of Old World or New World representatives they were his property. In fact the validity of the slave owner's rights even in the Northern States was affirmed by the mid-1850's when Melville submitted the story. The celebrated cases of Thomas Sims and Anthony Burns, fugitive slaves returned

62

by federal law to Southern masters, reversed earlier decisions including the U.S. Supreme Court judgment freeing the black insurgents who had won control of the Spanish ship _Amistad_, some fifteen years earlier.

Melville's audience should have known of and been conditioned by these aspects of the historical and legal context. The majority probably agreed with these legal vindications of property rights and were not at all prepared to encounter in a magazine story a challenge to, rather than a confirmation of, what they already believed. They might also have recognized some similarity between Alexandro Aranda's benevolence toward his slaves--leaving them unchained aboard the _San Dominick_ because he was confident of their tractability--and the case of Nat Turner, who turned the opportunities offered by a "generous" master into the staging ground for massive insurrection. Melville consciously enlarged the role of Aranda from the original narrative to emphasize the liberal master's underestimation of the slaves' desire for freedom and just as consciously changed the ship's name and set the date back to 1799 to coincide with the insurrection on Santo Domingo, not only the site of one of Columbus' first landings but also of the first European settlement and of the first large-scale import of African labor into the New World. These latter changes alone are enough to challenge the views of critics who would censure Melville for his insensitivity to slavery as well as those who say that the issue of race and slavery is only incidental to Melville's concern with abstract evil.

Aranda's benevolent despotism and costly miscalculation are replicated in the genial condescension and bland overconfidence of Amasa Delano in regard to blacks. Don Alexandro misjudged, as it were, the moral, political, and psychological nature of the knot he helped fashion and the error cost him his life. Amasa Delano is blind to the intertwined issues of domination and subjugation, civilization and the primitive, authority and liberty, and associated strands of cultural difference. He is locked into his preconceptions as securely as Atufal, the proud giant, seems locked into his chains, but paradoxically, even after the mystery is unlocked for Delano, he has still not solved the knot. Defeated, like Aranda, by its complexity, he nevertheless survives--ironically protected by the degree of his misperception. He is a man for whom believing is seeing, and in a setting where the sea is "like waved lead," the sky "a gray surtout," he is still confident of his standing with God and his knowledge of men. Trying to penetrate the opacities and rationalize the deceptions, Delano wanders the decks of the San Dominick with all the ingenuousness of a midshipman experiencing the Encantadas for the first time. Lacking the moral and mental instrumentalities, insensitive to irony and ambiguity, he tries to follow the charts he had learned to sail by through waters more troubled than he could possibly imagine. He trusts his liberal sympathies, his tolerant generosity, and his self-righteous certainties to guide him. Many of Melville's readers have moved through the opacities of the story in the same misguided way.

Delano cannot conceive of how a good man could do bad, he sees suffering and misery as resulting providentially from vice, and in a cultural corollary to the work ethic he links the lack of competence, precision, and order aboard the San Dominick to the moral default of Old World Spain, where position is due more to noble birth than ability or achievement. Stock responses and often contradictory stereotypes betray him repeatedly as he misconstrues or only partially recognizes the symbolic import of sword, flag, or chains. These have traditional associations which he can share, but he cannot approach the full meaning of the shrouded figurehead, rotting balustrade, or enigmatic stern-piece. The latter, carved with the castle and lion of Spain, bears "a dark satyr in a mask, holding his foot on the prostrate neck of a writhing figure, likewise masked" (259). Delano cannot even associate this master-slave symbol with his idea of the relationship between Cereno and Babo. After the legal deposition more fully acquaints him (and us) with Cereno's viewpoint and experience, he can listen to but not share Cereno's reversal of the symbolized roles. Delano's firm belief in Negro simple-mindedness, his acceptance of the legend of the loyal body servant, his acquiescence with the concept of slave as extension of the master's will, and his generous acceptance of the burden of white paternalism drain the symbol of its initial meaning as well as its ironic reversal, and abort the possibility of his recognizing his own participation in this account of the controvertibility of roles and the ambiguity of evil. And it is not likely that most of Melville's readers, sharing many of Delano's assumptions, see any deeper into the events than he can. Thrust suddenly into the dramatic action, Delano is described "with scales dropped from his eyes," but the full epiphanic irony of the stern-piece lies in Delano's new position in the symbolic tableau--clutching the terrified Spaniard with his left hand while "his right foot . . . ground the prostrate negro" into the bottom of the small boat (327-38). He is a heraldic representative of America triumphant over decadent Europe and backward Africa. Unwittingly but effectively, Delano constitutes Melville's discerning announcement of New World imperialism replacing the enfeebled authority of Old World imperial force.

For the audience to recognize the full extent of Delano's shallowness and perceptual limitations would involve many of them unwillingly in mocking themselves and acknowledging the arrogance of their own assumptions. Most would rather ignore the irony of Delano's tenuous cloak of self-assurance as he half imagines his danger in the hands of the pitiably impotent Spaniard whom he misconstrues as a cruel master and capricious pirate: "Who would murder Amasa Delano? His conscience is clean. There is some one above" (298). In all likelihood, more readers were guilty of the same arrogance of innocence as Amasa Delano: the genteel presumptuousness that the internalized concepts of his culture enabled him to comprehend the world and speak with certainty of God's will and the inner nature of other men and women. These cultural concepts were to divine design like print and seal, assuring that the world of man and nature was programmed into lawful patterns and orderly processes. Founded on extravagant promise, this New World faith was expressed in expectation not in recollection. In his summary comments to Benito Cereno, Delano stresses the power of "yon bright sun" to forget, of "the blue sea, and the blue sky" to restore themselves, of "these mild trades" to heal--nature constantly nourishing, sustaining, restoring (352). Without having read Emerson, Delano knew that the world existed for man; without Thoreau's guidance he lived in the infinite expectation of the dawn.

In contrast to Delano's gospel of faith, hope and confidence, Cereno speaks from the painful depths of his experience--a gospel of memory that relives the agony without the resurrection. In moral terms, the story is a virtual standoff: the American's technical competence and intellectual infantilism matched against the Spaniard's physical enervation and pathetic incapacitation. Only Babo—resourceful in life, stubbornly silent at his trial, unabashed even in death—combines all the human attributes of a tragic hero. But he could not be cast in such a role from a New World or an Old World perspective, and in Melville's time the Third World lacked an adequate voice or a significant vote.

We can assume that many readers also shared Delano's covert prejudices against Spain and the Spanish presence in the New World, linking anti-Catholic sentiments and anti-monarchist feelings with Spanish decadence, colonial maladministration, and resistance to progress—the Protestant Ethic become foreign policy and justifying American responsibility for removing incompetent authority in a foreign principality. Similarly, they could share his recurrent suspicions of Benito Cereno as sinister conspirator or torpid invalid unfit to command, while almost simultaneously trying to expel these fears through an open-handed, democratic diminution and acceptance of ethnic differences: "These Spaniards are all an odd set; the very word Spaniard has a curious, conspirator, Guy-Fawkish twang to it. And yet, I dare say, Spaniards in the main are as good folks as any in Duxbury, Massachusetts" (300). It is highly unlikely that Melville's audience could recognize that either of Delano's assumptions (one expressed in clearly prejudicial terms, the other in specious egalitarianism) impeded effective communication. Despite his knowledge of Spanish, Delano could never understand anyone of Cereno's background, much less his predicament. In fact, applied social science labors to make explicit in 1975 what was so implicit to Melville about intercultural communication in 1855. Consider the following passage taken from a current Department of State publication and based on research performed under contract with the Department of the Army:

> It is virtually impossible for anyone to communicate with other people without making assumptions about them. We may make these assumptions knowingly or, more commonly, without being aware of making them. Ease of communication is determined, in part, by the extent to which such assumptions are correct.

When false assumptions interfere with communication, we may recognize that this is happening. We may sometimes discover later that it has occurred. Frequently, we never become aware of it.

Our assumptions about other people can be traced to a variety of causal factors. Of particular importance in intercultural encounters are assumptions that are the result of our own cultural conditioning. The effects of that conditioning on our thought processes can be quite subtle, making it difficult to recognize the resulting assumptions for what they are. Often such assumptions manifest themselves as <u>projected cognitive similarity</u>--that is, when we implicitly assume that the other person's ideas and thought processes are similar to what ours would be if we were in their place.[5]

Toward Babo, Delano does not attempt the social and psychological equivalency of "projected cognitive similarity"; but in regard to Benito Cereno, it is Captain Delano's tranquilizer, beclouding his perception of what the Spaniard is going through and the meaning of what he has been through.

Many readers, however, construe Benito Cereno's physical and psychological trauma, his tortured recognition of evil, as the central meaning of the story, and some even go so far as to identify Cereno with Melville, who they feel was similarly appalled by the immediacy of evil. This identification further assumes the author's approbation of Cereno's attitude and outlook and ignores his effeteness, impotence, and inability to confront the world as it is. His monastic withdrawal, as R. H. Fogle has pointed out, is no more adequate or admirable a way of dealing with the world than is the carefree bachelor approach of Amasa Delano. The two men are as opposed to each other in their conceptions of the world as the two sides of a Galapagos tortoise, and their confrontation leads only to surface communication. They remain forever blocked from any benefit from each other's strength or insight, morally or psychologically crippled by their own incompleteness. If Amasa Delano lives in an ambiance of benign expectation, unscarred by pain and misery, Benito

Cereno lives with the agony of his experience, his memory the ceaseless nightmare of his present existence. The American is a historical amnesiac untroubled by the past; the Spaniard a much-troubled victim of physical and spiritual trauma.

From its original figurehead, honoring the agent of Spain who discovered the New World, to Benito Cereno's unhappy retreat and death in the monastery of Mount Agonia, to the legalized barbarism of Babo's execution (his head "fixed on a pole in the Plaza, met, unabashed, the gaze of the whites"), the drama on the San Dominick has telescoped three centuries of Spanish history (353). Melville's view of these circumstances anticipates that of Carlos Fuentes, who argues that the forces "that killed the promise of freedom and love and joy in Spain," that produced Spanish decadence and impotence "began in the instant of Spanish glory." Connecting the climactic discovery of the New World and the crest of the Inquisition in 1492, he asserts that the misguided attempt to strengthen "national unity, Catholic faith, and purity of blood . . . out of love for Christ and his Holy Mother" inevitably launched Spain on a course of degeneracy, withdrawal, and isolation:

> The hollow imperial gesture, by which Spain defeated herself, fatally cut herself off from the human, cultural and economic resources that fled with the expulsion of the Jews and the defeat of the Arabs.

Of course, this view asserts more than Melville includes, but Fuentes' image of a nation fruitlessly "fighting against the Reformation," living with a self-imposed "quarantine . . . against the diseases of modernity," worshiping the symbols of "honor, purity, and orthodoxy," fashioning "verbal masks . . . to uphold appearances" while its aristocratic dynasties faded "into insanity, hemophilia, syphillis, frivolity and . . . idiocy," can deepen a contemporary reader's understanding of Cereno's weakness, withdrawal, and death.[6]

Fuentes' phrases effectively gloss Melville's imagistic description of the San Dominick as "a white-washed monastery" with "Black Friars pacing the cloisters." (The Dominicans, or Black Friars, were prominent sponsors of the Inquisition.) Other details such as the "slovenly neglect," the "Dry Bones," and "hearse-like" aspect of the ship, the state-cabin windows "hermetically closed and calked," the numerous signs of "faded grandeur," further fit into Fuentes' argument. And even the Spanish captain's behavior and appearance--his "saturnine mood of ill-health," "his national formality," his "mental disorder," his "unstrung," "half-lunatic" state of mind--exemplify Fuentes' charges against the Spanish aristocracy (257-65). The fading grandeur and structural rot of the San Dominick contrasts with the power and pride once conveyed by its heraldic castle and lion, and Don Benito is as much a relic as that fading crest, leaning weakly on contrivance and appearance to stiffen the semblance of authority.

This view of Spanish history might also help a modern reader, blessed with greater sophistication in regard to verbal masks and legalistic deceit, see the lengthy legal deposition as a contrived cover-up rather than a revelation, for the deposition clearly expresses the values and reinforces the status-quo of the Spanish colonial establishment, ignoring Spanish injustices and black aspirations, glossing over the civilized savagery of the Spanish to condemn black barbarities, and views that somewhat indiscriminate massacre of blacks and Spaniards by Delano's SWAT force ("nearly a score of negroes were killed," none of the Americans) as a fortunate victory. Thus, the legalistic expression of the establishment view, in its intent to reveal the "true history of the San Dominick's voyage" (333), communicates a socially acceptable fiction--a device Melville also employs at the end of Billy Budd where the historical record is left with an account of how the mutinous foreigner Budd stabbed the patriotic Claggart and was duly executed for his crime.

The deposition follows the narrative as if to unlock its mysteries, clarify its deceptions, and offer reassurance about the quality of justice. But the more attentive reader recognizes that the complexities of the knot have not been solved, even though Melville has served up a key to fit the padlocked narrative. Like Atufal's shackles, the locked-up truth in the narrative remains enchained only as long as the victim, or victimized reader, participates in the deception. The deposition thus wraps the reader in new coils of deception as it seems to unwrap the old. The key in this instance is that no man is merely a spectator, that significant art compels participation and engagement before it yields enlightenment, and that the reader in his approach to experience (including the experience of art) ultimately has the means to his own liberation.

Modern readers might also have some more associations with which to construct a context for "Benito Cereno." If they knew that the leader of the Amistad mutineers was a black known as Cinque or Cinquez, they could confront the ironic emergence in the 1970's of a black insurrectionist who took that name in espousing his violent, prison-spawned version of liberation. Such an irony underscores not only Santayana's dictum about those ignorant of the past doomed to relive it but also how close to savagery the civilized authorities of Chicago or Los Angeles can be, in subduing the Panthers or the Symbionese, to the colonial authorities of early nineteenth-century Lima.

I was myself surprised to discover that the real Amasa Delano, whose name echoes through recent American history in the annals of one of our near-dynastic families, as well as the site of a domestic third-world confrontation in the California grape fields, should have been an early pioneer of pan-American foreign policy and cross-cultural understanding. And in another compounding of ironic associations, I thought of how a prominent American official has had his goodwill missions to Latin America marred by the jumble of painful reality and unlikely mythic allusion, replaying on the stage of an Attica prison yard the drama of the San Dominick. "Benito Cereno" is truly a story whose time has come, whose currency will not soon pass, and whose present readers must be encouraged to use their own knowledge and experience in undoing the knot that Melville's contemporaries were less equipped to handle.

1. The range of allegorical interpretation runs from identification of Cereno as Melville the writer suffering the attacks of hostile critics, to Cereno as metaphorical embodiment of Charles the Fifth betrayed by black deeds of the Church in Spain, to Cereno as representative of Spanish colonial policy and the slaveholding establishment. Babo thus ranges from malicious literary critic or sadistic agent of the Spanish Inquisition or overt devil to heroic freedom-fighter. While there is greater consensus regarding the character of Delano as representative American, there are some significant differences in assessing his relative strengths and limitations.

Much of the pertinent criticism is included or listed in two collections with a similar purpose. Both reprint the pertinent chapter from Amasa Delano's account of the experience underlying "Benito Cereno" and both contain selected and annotated bibliographies: (1) _A Benito Cereno Handbook_, ed. Seymour L. Gross (Belmont, 1965) and (2) _Melville's Benito Cereno_, ed. John P. Runden (Boston, 1965). Some important subsequent articles are listed in _Eight American Authors_, ed. James Woodress (New York, 1971), and in the recent annual compilations of _American Literary Scholarship_ (Durham, 1963-).

2. All page references to "Benito Cereno" are keyed to Jay Leyda's edition of _The Complete Stories of Herman Melville_ (New York, 1949).

3. _The Profession of Authorship in America_, 1800-1870, ed. Matthew J. Bruccoli (Columbus, 1968), p. 211.

4. From "Hawthorne and His Mosses," in _Billy Budd and Other Prose Pieces_, ed. Raymond W. Weaver (New York, 1963), p. 131.

5. Alfred J. Kraemer, "Cultural Self-Awareness and Communication," _International Educational and Cultural Exchange_, 10, No. 3 (Winter 1975), 13.

6. Fuentes' remarks appeared in the course of a review of _Count Julian_, by Juan Goytisolo, in _The New York Times Book Review_, 79, No. 18 (May 5, 1974), 5.

THE CENTRALITY OF WALT WHITMAN

It was during a two-year period of teaching abroad that I became aware of the very considerable foreign interest in Walt Whitman. Gradually I realized that these students who were curious enough about our culture to study our language and to probe our literature recognized Whitman as a unique spokesman for nineteenth-century America and, even more dramatically, they find his work offers a means of testing American values in the twentieth century. Since then I have also spoken to Roger Asselineau about his initial attraction to Whitman's poetry, an attraction that began when, in his words, France was "one vast concentration camp" and Whitman offered vistas of freedom, if only in the imagination.

In Whitman's revolt against metrical restraints in poetry, in his hostility to traditional forms, in his stridently democratic egalitarianism, these European students of American literature see a poetic parallel to the unprecedented American political experiment based on the inalienable rights of man and denouncing the wrongs of traditional authority, whether social, political, or religious. (Asian students, as might be expected, are more drawn to the mystical and meditative strains in his poetry.) His expansiveness, his vulgar lack of refinement, and his egotism echo the mood of a people on the march and with a mission--to subdue the wilderness, to extend the frontier, to harness the water power, to mine the resources, to create the manufacturing complex that would amaze the world--in short, to demonstrate in every sense the material as well as the moral superiority of being an American during the period that has belatedly been recognized and labelled as our industrial "take-off."

This period of our most startling and extensive industrial growth, roughly from 1843 to 1857, is also that which students of literature have come to call "the American Renaissance," following F. O. Matthiessen's lead. It was a time in which Emerson felt "life was made over anew," a time of accelerating change which produced <u>The Scarlet Letter</u>, <u>Moby Dick</u>, <u>Walden</u>, as well as <u>Leaves of Grass</u>. The character of the times, I would insist, is electrically conveyed in these works, especially in the imaginative conjunction of emotion, experience, and idea and in the frequently stunning resort to strategies of symbolism to deal with circumstances that literary tradition could not encompass.

To return, though, to the European who sees Whitman as the best representative of the promise, the strength, and the novelty that were integral to the American experiment at mid-century. It does not require any kind of sinister conspiracy to alert this student--whose interest in things American is usually based in sympathy or admiration--to alert him to the discrepancy between the democratic vision of Whitman, linking races, creeds, and occupations, and the denials of freedom that punctuate American history. Only a decade ago, headlines describing events in obscure Mississippi towns vied in importance in foreign newspapers with reports of the fall of governments, and even our best friends abroad could not adequately answer the critics who asked how the nation which saw itself leading the free world could countenance such denials of freedom at home and initiate such a misguided policy in southeast Asia. The facts were clearly at odds with Whitman's vision of the magnificent moral giants, simultaneously crude, common, and sensitive, who are _en masse_ the American people. And in an ironic, even paradoxical way, the discrepancy between Whitman's vision of America and current reality swelled the tide of anti-Americanism that seems to wash repeatedly through much of Europe.

I

Whitman's "Song of Myself" conspicuously celebrates the absence of class distinctions, the ready acceptance of change, and the way the resultant fluidity, flexibility, and familiarity enable millions of strong, discrete individuals to mesh their wills and merge their personalities in a spiritual as well as a political Union. His "Passage to India" sings of the miracles of technology which will overcome the barriers that separate men, nations, continents--those material miracles that for Whitman symbolize men's spiritual discovery of their shared origins and objectives. And again the contemporary reality contradicts Whitman's idealistic vision, for these modern miracles that bring men into closer proximity--in Whitman's time the symbolic golden spike, Atlantic cable, and Suez Canal--can just as easily dramatize the differences that proximity cannot overcome. Our communications satellites and space endeavors produce more international suspicion than shared interests. Despite Detente the hot line between Washington and Moscow is, of course, a holdover from the cold war and no one can take encouragement from thinking about the occasion which may require the next person-to-person call. Even the physical presence of so many thousands of Americans abroad facilitates too little communication of a desirable sort. The American tourist, booked into a Hilton hotel in Istanbul, or Athens, or Paris, the military and diplomatic personnel with their network of commissaries, PX's, and AFEX's have been too often isolated in ghettoes of affluence, almost completely enslaved by their need to have their hamburgers, cokes, martinis, frozen orange juice, and peanut butter wherever they go.

But we should not forget that as Americans we have strengths as well as shortcomings. A few years ago, borrowing a phrase from Henry James, a British critic very aptly termed it "a complex fate" to be an American, but he was rather condescending--mistakenly, I think.[1] It is a complex fate but also a significant achievement to be an American, and it requires some knowledge of the ideas and values which are part of our history and some knowledge also of the men who gave them effective expression. And in this regard we can learn from examining Whitman as a man shaped by American circumstances and in his own right a shaper of a significant segment of American thought.

It was a European student, oddly enough, who predicted the emergence of the kind of poet that Whitman was and based his prediction not on the literature he actually read in America but on the implications that democratic social theory held for the development of culture in general. Fully twenty years before Whitman published his Leaves of Grass, Alexis de Tocqueville, in his unsurpassed study of Democracy in America noted that the young republic had yet no poetry worthy of the name; but, insisting that democratic theory was not inherently hostile to poetry, only to the kind of poetry produced in the aristocratic past, Tocqueville tried to imagine the general contours and special concerns of this still unconceived poetry. Extrapolating freely from what he observed in the areas of politics and the professions, in the character of the laws and the behavior of the people, Tocqueville surmised that "in democratic communities, where men are all insignificant and very much alike, each man instantly sees all his fellows when he surveys himself." And since he also felt that democracy, unlike aristocracy, "gives men a sort of instinctive distaste for what is ancient" and fosters ideas of progress and human perfectibility, democratic poets would "care but little for what has been, but instead they are haunted by visions of what will be. . . . Democracy, which shuts the past against the poet, opens the future before him." New themes and new techniques, Tocqueville insisted, are inevitable:

> As all the citizens who compose a democratic community are nearly equal and alike, the poet cannot dwell upon any one of them; but the nation itself invites the exercise of his powers. The general similitude of individuals, which renders any one of them taken separately an improper subject of poetry, allows poets to include them all in the same imagery, and to take a general survey of the people itself. Democratic nations have a clearer perception than any others of their own aspect; and an aspect so imposing is admirably fitted to the delineation of the ideal.

The mobility of the people, both in a social and in a geographical sense tends ultimately, he suggested, to minimize differences so that "it is not only . . . the members of the same community who grow more alike; communities themselves are assimilated to one another, and the whole assemblage presents to the eye of the spectator one vast democracy, each citizen of which is a nation." And as a consequence, "All that belongs to the existence of the human race taken as a whole, to its vicissitudes and its future, becomes an abundant mine of poetry." Discarding legend, tradition, and supernatural heroes, the poet of the new age will concentrate on "man himself, taken aloof from his country and his age and standing in the presence of Nature and of God, with his passions, his doubts, his rare prosperities and inconceivable wretchedness."[2]

To explain such remarkably accurate prophecy, one must either believe in miracles or acknowledge a vital relation between Whitman's poetry and conditions of life in America, as observed and interpreted in this instance by a sensitive social scientist who also knew his humanities.

Closer to home, we can also find oracular indications of the direction Whitman would follow. In an essay composed in the early 1840's, Emerson defined the role of the poet who would deal adequately with the American challenge and explore the character of contemporary change, but confessed that neither he nor anyone else had so far met the demands:

We do not with sufficient plainness or sufficient profoundness address ourselves to life, nor dare we chaunt our own times and social circumstances. . . . Time and nature yield us many gifts, but not yet the timely man, the new religion, the reconciler, whom all things await. Dante's praise is that he dared to write his autobiography in colossal cipher, or into universality. We have yet had no genius in America with tyrannous eye, which knew the value of our incomparable materials, and saw, in the barbarism and materialism of the times, another carnival of the same gods whose picture he so much admires in Homer; then in the Middle Ages; then in Calvinism. Banks and tariffs, the newspaper and the caucus, Methodism and Unitarianism, are flat and dull to dull people, but rest on the same foundation of wonder as the town of Troy and the Temple of Delphi. . . . Our log-rolling, our stumps and their politics, our fisheries, our Negroes and Indians, our boa[s]ts and our repudiations, the wrath of rogues and the pusillanimity of honest men, the northern trade, the southern planting, the western clearing, Oregon and Texas, are yet unsung. Yet America is a poem in our eyes; its ample geography dazzles the imagination, and it will not wait long for meters.

When the first edition of _Leaves of Grass_ appeared in 1855, Emerson's reaction was instantaneous: "I greet you at the beginning of a great career, which yet must have had a long foreground somewhere, for such a start. I rubbed my eyes a little, to see if this sunbeam were no illusion; but the solid sense of the book is a sober certainty."[3]

II

Emerson referred to the "long foreground" which he felt must have led to <u>Leaves of Grass</u>. It is this foreground which shaped Whitman in the American mold, which made him the extravagant culmination of a cultural process which began even before the United States had a national identity. With the Puritans' intent to establish a New Jerusalem where the individual sinner might undergo a spiritual regeneration, which would permit his joining the community of saints, the Elect of God, wilderness America had been given a role and the new American a rare opportunity. When Benjamin Franklin, seventeen years old, stepped ashore in Philadelphia, one Dutch dollar in his pocket, but the virtually unlimited opportunity of the New World before him, he exemplified the secular possibilities of the American condition. His rise "from the poverty and obscurity" of his birth "to a state of affluence and some degree of reputation in the world" is a story of moral triumph as well as material success, and the purpose of his <u>Autobiography</u> is to demonstrate that every citizen of the New World has access to the same realm of promise by virtue of his being a citizen in this new land of promise. St. Jean de Crevecoeur, in a famous letter, asked "What is the American, this new man?" And he found his answer not only in the amalgamation of diverse ethnic strains already visible in the 1780's but especially in the unique conditions which in their unprecedented liberality sanctioned social change and provided "this new man" with every opportunity for a fresh start. So enamored was Jefferson of this right of every man to step clear of the past in shaping his life and his society, that he seriously wondered how it could be effectively legislated. His call for a major upheaval every nineteen years with a complete reformulation of the law was based on no fondness for disorder or bloodletting but on his conviction that each generation be entitled to stand free of the bonds of the past and construct a world to meet its changing needs. Emerson himself insisted that what the first man could do, every American could also do, and he referred not to original sin but to the original opportunity to begin with a clean slate. "The sun shines today also," he wrote, urging the self-reliant American to cast off his intellectual bondage to the past. His object was to indicate the possibility of spiritual rebirth and the original vigor which would result. Thoreau no less seriously created a distinctly American fable of rebirth, new beginnings, fresh discoveries. Everything in the structure and the imagery of Walden-- with its pattern of seasonal renewal and its attention to snakes sloughing off the old skin, Indians purifying themselves by burning their possessions (their bondage to the past) in a ritual busk, Thoreau's own baptism in his morning dip in the pond, the innumerable examples of dormant nature awakening to new life--all those unmistakably convey Thoreau's message, define the most distinctive condition of the American experience, and supply a powerful mythology for a people striving to reconcile enterprise and idealism. This is part of that "long foreground" which enabled Whitman to stand forth as an American Adam, an original man, in his eyes the first man to write the poetry and reveal the character of the new man and the new world.

And in this sense the vein of political rhetoric that has given us in the twentieth century the successive promises of the New Freedom and the New Deal and the New Frontier runs deeper than the sloganeers may realize, for these words indicate a continuing need to vitalize the crucial meaning of the American experience.

It is not simply the fact that in America the President takes off his hat to the people "not they to him" that excites Whitman. It is rather the hopeful and confident air of a people who in their exodus from Europe shed their burden of guilt and doubt, who in their repudiation of the European experience gambled on the certainty of a new genesis, and who in terms of their triumph remain the perpetually youthful and innocent protagonists in the myth of a continuing genesis, making a virtue of constant change and positing perpetually new beginnings and fresh opportunities. His "Song of Myself" proclaims our emancipation from history and sets our moral course not in terms of recreation of, or readjustment to, or identification with the past, nor in any terms of necessary redemption, but in outspoken and uninhibited terms of the healthy exercise of unimpaired, natural faculties. Asserting repeatedly that there should be no shame in the body, no repression of the emotions, no censor to the mind, and no barrier to the soul, Whitman celebrates the miracle of democratic man and tries to demonstrate that "the United States themselves are essentially the greatest poem."

III

In stressing the superiority of what was natural in feeling and expression, Whitman consciously rejected what was imitative, artificial, conventional, or traditional in poetry. And in the process he created a new persona and fashioned a new style, a word which I use to suggest more than the way words are used to articulate a thought, but rather a mode of thought itself. We look upon Whitman, as we look upon Mark Twain, as one of the shapers of modern American writing for just this reason: his vernacular mode has become a national style, not only an American way of writing and thinking which differentiates English and American literature, but an American way of dressing, of housing, of teaching, or of running for political office. This style is not necessarily good because it is American; it is in fact an index to the dangers as well as the possibilities of democratic society. But before I say more about the dangers or the liabilities, let me illustrate this style, this new point of view that Walt Whitman brought to poetry.

I am indebted for this example to one of my former teachers, Professor Leo Marx, now at MIT, and I continue to rely on it because I find it such an admirably effective clarification. During the years that Whitman's poetry was, in his own word, "simmering," another rather special American subject was approaching a boil--the problem of slavery. It is not surprising that many of Whitman's contemporaries had also treated this subject in poetry, but poetry of a traditional kind. Here is a good example by the popular poet of the time, Henry Wadsworth Longfellow:

The Slave in the Dismal Swamp

In dark fens of the Dismal Swamp
  The hunted Negro lay;
He saw the fire of the midnight camp,
And heard at times a horse's tramp
  And a bloodhound's distant bay.

Where will-o-the-wisps and glow-worms shine,
  In bulrush and in brake;
Where waving masses shroud the pine,
And the cedar grows, and the poisonous vine
  Is spotted like the snake;

Where hardly a human foot could pass,
  Or a human heart would dare,
On the quaking turf of the green morass
He crouched in the rank and tangled grass
  Like a wild beast in his lair.

A poor old slave, infirm and lame;
  Great scars deformed his face;
On his forehead he bore the brand of shame,
And the rags, that hid his mangled frame,
  Were the livery of disgrace.

All things above were bright and fair,
  All things wee glad and free;
Lithe squirrels darted here and there,
And wild birds filled the echoing air
  With songs of Liberty!

On him alone was the doom of pain,
  From the morning of his birth;
On him alone the curse of Cain
Fell, like a flail on the garnered grain,
  And struck him to earth!

If we set beside Longfellow's poem some lines from Section 10 of "Song of Myself," we may note the significant differences:

The runaway slave came to my house and stopt outside,
I heard his motions crackling the twigs of the woodpile,
Through the swung half-door of the kitchen I saw him limpsy and weak,

And went where he sat on a log and led him in and
assured him.
And brought water and fill'd a tub for his sweated
body and bruis'd feet,
And gave him a room that enter'd from my own, and
gave him some coarse, clean linen clothes,
And remember perfectly well his revolving eyes and
his awkwardness,
And remember putting plasters on the galls of his
neck and ankles;
He staid with me a week before he was recuperated
and pass'd north,
I had him sit next me at table, my fire-lock lean'd
in the corner.

Even if some readers prefer Longfellow's to Whitman's
poem (in fact I would be surprised if some did not deny
that Whitman's lines were even poetry), the basis for
their judgment is an indication of Whitman's new role
and voice. They may insist that Longfellow's lines
sound like poetry and on the page have the recognizable
appearance of poetry, and I would have to agree, before
pointing out that what sounds "poetic" was already by
the mid-nineteenth century an imitative and shopworn
literary language. This is the very apparatus that
Whitman had to abandon in his effort to get close to
his subject. Not only is the diction different, but
Whitman has dispensed with meter and rhyme. He has
even dispensed with the poet. In Longfellow's poem we
can see the traditional calling of the poet. Our
attention is drawn not to the actual circumstances of a
slave in a swamp, but to a man using the special equipment reserved for men of letters when they write poems.
In Whitman's lines, however, the poet does not obtrude;
he just about disappears, for the "I" of Whitman's poem
is simultaneously the hero and the poet. This persona,
the first-person narrator, results in a new sort of
immediacy. The poem becomes less of an intellectual
exercise and more of a distinctly human experience.
And the key to this is of course the language of the
poem.

   I do not mean that Whitman's language was literally the speech of the streets; indeed it was not. Without reproducing the spoken language of the time,
Whitman still manages to create the illusion that a
certain recognizable kind of man is speaking, someone
who can say

> I wear my hat as I please indoors or out.
> Why should I pray? Why should I venerate and be
> ceremonious?
> Having pried through the strata, analyzed to a
> hair, counsel'd with doctors and calculated
> close,
> I find no sweeter fat than sticks to my own bones.

The illusion stems, I suspect, more from the cadence--
which is there, despite the lack of any traditional
meter or rhyme--than from the diction. The lines come
closer to the spoken language than any previous American poetry because Whitman is trying to find a vital
way of conveying ideas and emotions for which the standard poetic manner was inappropriate. Think back to
those two poems again:

> In dark fens of the Dismal Swamp
> The hunted Negro lay;

and Whitman:

> I heard his motions crackling the twigs of the
> woodpile,
> Through the swung half-door of the kitchen I saw
> him limpsy and weak.

Which man really saw the Negro? The answer lies in the
extraordinary sense of immediacy that the vernacular
mode can convey. Longfellow saw his subject through a
haze of trite images: "like a wild beast in his lair,"
"the brand of shame," "the livery of disgrace"; when
they are not tired, the phrases are pompous and inflat-
ed and further extend the distance between the poet and
his subject. To Whitman this slave was a man with
"sweated body and bruis'd feet." Longfellow says
"great scars deformed his face"; Whitman remembers
"putting plasters on the galls of his neck and ankles."
Whitman is not simply being more specific than Longfellow; he imagines a far different relation to the
Negro, and his use of the vernacular is far more than a
language experiment. It is the expression of a man
"hankering, gross, mystical, nude." Aggressively un-
conventional (where convention means an artificial or
genteel form of thought and behavior), he is the level-
ing force of Jacksonian democracy out to tumble the
proud and raise the humble:

In all people I see myself, none more and not one a
    barley-corn less,
And the good or bad I say of myself I say of them.

Combining egotism and egalitarianism, realism and mysticism, in this kind of hero, he extends the limits of
poetry and propriety. His vernacular view is far more
candid than the traditional pose of the poet and enables him to try new things thematically as well as
technically: to deal with the life and quality of the
burgeoning cities, to develop a stream of consciousness
that is at times tender and at times tough, to treat
love and sex with unprecedented frankness, to avoid
a priori judgments, to hang loose.

Many readers object to what they term Whitman's
overstatement, his lack of subtlety, but they overlook
a kind of subtlety that also stems from the use of a
vernacular narrator, who, like Huck Finn, is so integral a part of the experience described. Longfellow
told us repeatedly that his Negro was "hunted," men-
tioning in successive lines the "horse's tramp," the
"bloodhound's distant bay," finally that "on him alone
the curse of Cain / Fell. . . ." Whitman does not find
it necessary to instruct us in the same way. After
describing the matter-of-fact relations between the
narrator and the slave, he mentions casually, at the
end, his gun leaning in the corner. I am amazed when
some of my American students cannot tell me the meaning
of this final remark or suggest the gun is there because the narrator, while he sits next to the slave at
the table, does not fully trust him. Perhaps this
shows how far some of us are from Whitman's vernacular
views and his democratic faith; it also shows why
teachers have to struggle so in teaching twentieth-
century poetry, which depends so much on that kind of
ironic understatement here employed by Whitman. To me
that gun in the corner says a lot more about Whitman's
relation to the slave and to the Fugitive Slave Law and
to humanity than do all of Longfellow's well-intended
literary abstractions.

The reason Whitman does not have to proclaim the
feeling of solidarity between the two men is that the
vernacular style enables him to describe it so vividly.
This style itself is appropriate because it is not
simply a vehicle for asserting egalitarian democratic
values; it is an expression of those values, of the

ideal human community of Whitman's imagination. The
style is organically linked with a political philosophy
which disregards established forms--whether ideas of
class and status or the traditional forms of litera-
ture--in favor of a radical program of freedom. This
is the strength of Whitman's vernacular expression.
The dangers of the vernacular mode, which I can here
only suggest, lie in the implicit chauvinism which
consistently links Europe with the rubbish heap of the
past, and in the implicit anti-intellectualism of this
flight from formal disciplines and the trained mind.

And what has been the effect of Whitman's radical-
ly utopian conception of democratic community on American society? The story of our own times reveals too
many sad discrepancies at home and abroad for me to
suggest that we have realized Whitman's ideal, and it
might be foolish to believe that we ever shall. But as
an ideal which links our past with our hope for the
future, it gives us a direction in which to move.

Still we would be selling Whitman short if we
believed that his only influence was in articulating a
still unattained ideal. There are the obvious influences on poets like Hart Crane or Carl Sandburg, on the
many others who have adopted Whitman's pose without his
particular philosophical commitment. Despite the disciplined and erudite character of T. S. Eliot's verse
and Eliot's rejection of much that Whitman stands for,
it could be argued that Whitman's impressionistic
descriptions of the urban scene, even more his use of
the self as an underlying mythic principle, made available the instruments so differently employed in The
Wasteland. But there are deeper ways in which Whitman's thought has shaped our national expression.

IV

When I asserted that Whitman's style was an
organic outgrowth of his view of the self and society,
I understated an aesthetic principle of great significance. Whitman found the germ of this principle in
Emerson's complaint that in the poetry of his time the
thought or the argument was secondary and the external
finish primary. Emerson insisted instead that "it is
not meters, but a meter-making argument that makes a
poem,--a thought so passionate and alive that like the

84

spirit of a plant or an animal it has an architecture of its own, and adorns nature with a new thing." In this view we have an aesthetic justification for disregarding the past, for no preconceived or traditional form can be superimposed on new thought and experience; the content or the argument must determine its own naturally appropriate form. "The quality of the imagination," Emerson said, "is to flow, and not to freeze," and Whitman tried to create poems which "show the free growth of metrical laws and bud from them as unerringly and loosely as lilacs or roses on a bush." There can be nothing artificial, nothing purely decorative: only "those ornaments can be allowed that conform to the perfect facts of the open air and that flow out of the nature of the work and come irrepressibly from it and are necessary to the completion of the work. Most works are most beautiful without ornament." This is a very demanding as well as liberating kind of artistic integrity, an insistence on structural honesty with explicit architectural overtones. In his 1855 preface to <u>Leaves of Grass</u>, Whitman announced, "I will not have in my writing any elegance or effect . . . to hang in the way between me and the rest like curtains," and the seed of this conviction was destined to flower in the mind and the work of one of our greatest architectural creators. Whitman's rebellion in poetry is paralleled by Louis Sullivan's later overthrow of both the authority of the "Classic Orders" and the dominance of tradition in the teaching and practice of architecture.

A book of poems can have a preface; rarely can a building be similarly introduced or explained. But Louis Sullivan, the man to whom Frank Lloyd Wright was so fortunately apprenticed, has traced the development of his thought in terms that specifically recall Whitman, the vernacular mode, and the organic principle. Whitman used to insist so on the uniqueness of the self that he repeatedly claims in his poetry, "I am untranslatable." Here in the words of Louis Sullivan is a kind of translation, nevertheless, that preserves the Emerson-Whitman tradition in our culture, if anthing so rebellious could be said to constitute a tradition:

Architectural art to be of contemporary immediate value must be <u>plastic</u>; all senseless
conventional rigidity must be taken out of it;
it must intelligently serve--it must not sup-

85

press. In this wise the forms under [the architect's] hand would grow naturally out of the needs and express them frankly, and freshly. This meant . . . that he would put to the test a formula he had evolved, through long contemplation of living things, namely that form follows function, which would mean, in practice, that architecture might again become a living art.4

Whitman, in an almost mystical merging of artist and work of art, told his readers that "whoever touches this book, touches a man." Less dramatically but with the same intent of organically identifying the cultural experience of the self with architectural creativity, Sullivan titled his book The Autobiography of an Idea. And Frank Lloyd Wright chose to use the term "Organic Architecture" to describe the work of his most creative period, before his late indulgence in fantasy and eclecticism.

There is one final aspect of organic theory that I want to mention in connection with Whitman's work. Normally, when a poem or a collection of poems is published, its form is finished, permanent. Leaves of Grass appeared as a volume of about 100 pages in 1855; by 1891-92 it had grown to more than 450 pages. Other editions had appeared in 1856, 1860, 1867, and 1881. Whitman himself was responsible for these editions, no two of which are identical. He was constantly revising. Just as Whitman's appearance changed in the frontispiece to each edition, there was change and growth in the poetry. As self-appointed interpreter of America, Whitman found there was not only change in himself but in his America too. The successive editions reflect the changing response of a fluid, unfrozen imagination to a very plastic subject, and they reflect also Whitman's self-conscious anxiety beneath the blatant and histrionic terms in which he often sings of America. This is why it is really a complex fate and a significant achievement to be an American-- because America is a fluctuating conception, an unfinished process, rather than a formalized and static state. We are reminded of this regularly as we see new automobiles roll out of Detroit, or as we examine the nature of the Constitution, which was intended to guide, occasionally to restrain excess, but never to immobilize.

There are always some who look for a single fixed pattern to explain American development or formulate the American personality. They might look to the experience of Walt Whitman who spent more than forty years trying to put America into his book, knowing that his synthesis could never be final. Today there are citizens trying to escape from the anxiety of not knowing for sure, trying to fix the American Way of Life to one or another combination of eternal verities. In their fear of change, they intensify the unfamiliarity and discomfort of what seems alien to a supposedly purer past. In short they try to simplify or avoid the complex fate of being an American. I am afraid that our past history promises them little chance of success. And I would suggest a lesson from Walt Whitman's discovery in poetry that yesterday's America was different from today's and tomorrow's will be still more different. As the late Professor Perry Miller pointed out, what was most American about Walt Whitman was that he did not seek to confine America to one philosophic or poetic pattern; furthermore that the kind of mentality that would confine the American way to a single mode of response--whether in politics, economics, literary form, religion, or morality--this is the attitude which, in the context of our national experience, is truly un-American.[5] This lesson could benefit some of our legislators too. It is too bad that poetry is no longer a prerequisite to politics.

ENDNOTES

1.   Marius Bewley, _The Complex Fate_ (London, 1952).

2.   Democracy in America, ed. by Phillip Bradley, 2 vols. (New York, 1945), V.II, pp. 77-81.

3.   The passage from Emerson's "The Poet" is available in many texts; the reaction to _Leaves of Grass_ is from Emerson's letter to Whitman, dated July 21, 1855.

4.   Louis Sullivan, _The Autobiography of an Idea_ (New York, 1949), pp. 257-8.

5.   Perry Miller, "The Shaping of the American Character," _NEQ_, XXVIII (1955), pp. 453-4.

V

PUDD'NHEAD WILSON: HALF A DOG IS WORSE THAN NONE*

I

Mark Twain's Pudd'nhead Wilson has puzzled and provoked critics who, for various reasons, need to find cause for praise or censure. Some even challenge the appropriateness of the title. Wright Morris, in his introduction to the Signet edition of Pudd'nhead Wilson, shrewdly suggests that the last three words of the novel constitute a better title, and he is right that "Down the River" echoes threateningly and ambiguously throughout the novel.[1] It would be no less apt, however, to suggest "A Dog's Life" as an improvement on Mark Twain's title. And there is even a sense in which the more than spectral fear of being sold down the river, the precarious condition of a dog's life, and Wilson's fateful remark solving the problem of a barking dog by killing half are symbolic equivalents.

As we see it, this grotesque and absurd exchange in Chapter I is the most important iconographic clue to the meaning of the novel:

> "I wish I owned half of that dog."
> "Why?" somebody asked.
> "Because I would kill my half" (p. 25).

These words have been frequently pointed out but never adequately explained. Usually the incident is dismissed as simply a means of alienating David Wilson from most of the community and blocking him from any meaningful pursuit of his legal career. Both George M. Spangler and James M. Cox, in two of the more illuminating analyses of the novel cite the rather incredible and unrealistically obtuse reaction from the witnesses to Wilson's capricious, latently vicious remark—witnesses who should have been familiar with this kind of rustic hyperbole.[2] Spangler explains this lapse in

*Originally published with Michael Elliott as co-author.

terms of his property thesis: "Wilson's low status is the result of his apparent failure to respect and understand the laws of property" (p. 32). He does view the incident symbolically, but discerns its major meaning in Wilson's disregard for the material value of anything he owned. That Wilson cannot comprehend the nature of property seems dubious in view of his demonstrated intelligence, his familiarity with legal and scientific matters, his conventional respect for the town's leading citizens and their spurious values, and his own prolonged quest for acceptance and success. Cox sees the remark as a veiled and symbolic threat to the values of this slaveholding society and with admirable insight discerns a relationship between the "invisible dog" (whose disagreeable barking jarred the tranquility of Dawson's Landing) and Tom Driscoll (the "invisible" slave whose flagrant amorality exposes the deceitful morality of the community) (pp. 234-36).

We agree with Mr. Spangler about Mark Twain's concern with those forces that have "a vitiating and reductive influence on human beings," but we see this influence resulting from widespread adherence to any idea that destroys integrity, artificially assigns identity, and breaks up the organic wholeness essential to the survival of almost any living creature or social entity. Common to Mark Twain's characterization of the novel as the result of a literary Caesarian, to his equally complex operation turning the original Siamese twins into the nearly identical dark-haired Luigi and light-haired Angelo, to the easily accomplished exchange of the nearly indistinguishable infants in Roxy's care, and to the innocent but ironic symbolism of Wilson's early remark about an audible but unseen dog, is the sense of sudden separation or violent severance. The book was created by an act of imaginative cutting loose from its sources and draws heavily from Mark Twain's long obsession with twins, intentional imposture, and accidentally confused identities. Deriving also from the dualities of his own psychological tendencies and artistic role, the novel is a semi-serious, semi-comic grotesque—half-revealing, half-concealing the traumatic divisions and gross cruelties of what we have come to call "Middle America." It is a partially intentional, partially intuitive analysis of what can happen when a supposedly organic community maintains a network of social fictions based on an inevitably deadly and socially divisive idea of human fractions.

Although the final version retains elements of the original farce in combination with a distinctly tragic view of the human condition, the meaning can hardly be called unclear when it is so repeatedly reinforced by suggestive description, conscious symbolism, narrative circumstance, and melodramatic characterization.

There are four elements in Wilson's statement that serve a strong structural, symbolic, and thematic function in the novel. Since Spangler has thoroughly examined the element of ownership and property, we would like to focus on the meanings that make up the idea of _dog_, the imaginative function of fractional division conveyed by reference to _half_ a dog, and the perverse violence implicit in the overt or covert act of killing a significant fraction of a living entity.

II

There is a marked difference between Mark Twain's use of dogs (and cats) in earlier works and in _Pudd'nhead Wilson_, and the difference is an indication of the change in his view of human possibilities. In such earlier works as _Roughing It_ and _The Adventures of Tom Sawyer_, there was an exuberant delight in the spontaneous antics of a dog in church or a cat calculatedly disrupting the genteel formalities of Examination Day at school (and exposing the false glitter of establishment values by snatching off the toupee which had concealed the previously gilded surface of the teacher's bald head). Even the overly proud town dog in Chapter V of _Roughing It_ participates in a charade wherein his frustrating pursuit of the wily coyote demonstrates the superiority of unpretentiously vernacular values over genteel establishment complacency. But there is an entirely different quality to the "well-fed, well-petted, and properly revered cat" so evident on many of the flower-laden ledges of whitewashed houses in Dawson's Landing. This cat has become an essential feature of the moral inertia of the Southern slaveholding establishment:

> stretched at full length, asleep and blissful, with her furry belly to the sun and a paw curved over her nose. Then that house was complete and its contentment and peace were made manifest to

the world by this symbol, whose testimony is infallible (pp. 21-22).

And the dog also fulfills a symbolic role in the orderly plan of this pre-Civil War, Middle-American society. He has become the long-suffering victim of callous and complacent cruelty--infallible testimony to the most helpless and servile aspect of the human condition.

The dog mentioned by garrulous Jim Blaine in the diffuse string of associations that make up the anecdote of "His Grandfather's Old Ram" was never in danger of being injured, as was Jim's Uncle Lem when he broke the fall of an Irishman with a hod full of bricks, because a dog would never consent to become such an instrument of Providence. He would not hold still long enough to become the victim of such a genteel rationalization of divine procedures. Neither in David Wilson's first reference to the unseen dog, nor in the several circumstances where "dog" is used metaphorically, can the "dog" get out from under the painful role assigned by social providence. The fate of the dog is throughout the novel a continuing analogy to the closed-in, helpless state of man--the victim of complex forces that constitute an irresistible social determinism. Implicit in much of Pudd'nhead Wilson is Mark Twain's recurrent question--What is man?--and the answer--nothing but a lowly dog--is well on the way to Mark Twain's bitterest image of man as microbe.

Most of the references linking man's fate and a dog's life draw from the common reservoir of community values in Dawson's Landing, no matter whether voiced by Roxy, Tom, Wilson, or the ironic narrator, and the epithet "dog" is applied most frequently but not exclusively to Tom Driscoll. One pattern of reference links the helplessness of a dog owned by a particular master and the similar subservience of a slave. The narrator launches this image early in the novel when he describes Percy Driscoll, who is angry about the disappearance of a small sum of money, as "a fairly humane man toward slaves and other animals" and "an exceedingly humane man toward the erring of his own race" (p. 30). The attitude thus described is racist in two senses. It does not merely distinguish between black and white human beings; it classifies slaves as part of a different, distinctly inferior species. Further

remarks make clear that for virtually all members of
this community, even the Negroes themselves, the race
to which the Blacks belonged was not the human race.
In describing the consequences of Roxy's substituting
her child for that of her master, Mark Twain constructs
a passage that not only links the condition of a slave
and that of a dog, but also stresses the violent severance of a natural bond and the common fate of slave and
dog as victims of a capricious owner--all the elements
of Wilson's cryptic, symbolic, and, as Mark Twain
termed it, "his fatal remark":

> She saw her darling gradually cease from being her
> son, she saw that detail perish utterly; all that
> was left was master--master, pure and simple, and
> it was not a gentle mastership, either. She saw
> herself sink from the sublime height of motherhood
> to the somber depths of slavery. The abyss of
> separation between her and her boy was complete.
> She was merely his chattel now, his convenience,
> his dog, his cringing and helpless slave, the
> humble and unresisting victim of his capricious
> temper and vicious nature (pp. 44-45).

After he learns of his true parentage, Tom Driscoll
also sees himself as a helpless figure in the property-
slave-dog pattern. Thinking of his foster-father, he
tells himself, "He is white; and I am his chattel, his
property, his goods, and he can sell me, just as he
could his dog" (p. 76).

As Tom applies this term to himself, it connotes
self-pity, not condemnation. As others address Tom in
terms that connect him with some alleged characteristic
of a dog, the meanings escalate in contempt and condemnation. There is even a kind of folk innocence in
Roxy's exclamation when she first switches the infants'
clothes and thereby their identities as well: "Dog my
cats if it ain't all I kin do to tell t'other fum
which" (p. 36). In a deeper sense, however, "dog my
cats" launches the confusion, the crime, and the chase
that form the main plot. The charges that Tom has a
viciously unhuman streak in him begin to pick up when
Roxy laughs at his attempt to club her in retaliation
for her revealing his ancestry to him: "Set down, you
pup! Does you think you kin skyer me?" (p. 71). When
Judge Driscoll calls Tom "You cur! You scum! You
vermin!" he is referring not to Tom's viciousness but

to his cowardice and lack of honor in turning to a court of law rather than the duel required by the F.F.V. code to remedy an insult (p. 96). Roxy makes the same charge when she concludes her fanciful genealogy linking Tom with his F.F.V. father, John Smith, Pocahontas, and "a nigger king outen Africa": "here you is, a slinkin' outen a duel en disgracin' our whole line like a ornery lowdown hound!" (p. 109).

By the time Tom initiates his plan to save himself by selling his mother, Roxy raises the charge against him from cowardice to superlative viciousness. Her first reaction upon escaping and confronting Tom is to detail the cruelties she had been through and try to shame Tom by saying "Sell a pusson down de river--<u>down de river</u>! . . . I wouldn't treat a dog so!" (p. 129). But she quickly learns that Tom is beyond shame or redemption, that he intends to profit further from her third return to slavery, and she charges him with the ultimate betrayal: "You could be Judas to yo' own mother to save yo' wuthless hide! Would anybody b'lieve it? No--a dog couldn't! You is de lowdownest orneriest hound dat was ever pup'd into dis worl'" (p. 136). As if to make sure the trebly-made point will not be lost, Mark Twain has Roxy repeat the charge a page later: "You's de lowdownest hound dat ever--but I done tole you dat befo'" (p. 137).

The final reference to "dog," like the first, stems from Wilson. Tom has dropped in on Wilson to gloat over what he is certain will be Luigi's impending conviction for the murder Tom has himself committed. Finding Wilson examining slides of fingerprints, Tom picks one up, sees Roxy's name on it and asks "Are you going to ornament the royal palaces with nigger paw marks, too?" His next remark is a further attempt to deny his natural relationship to Roxy and to project on to Chambers (the true Tom Driscoll) the subhuman animalistic qualities that his mother and foster-father have leveled at him: "By the date here, I was seven months old when this was done, and she was nursing me and her little nigger cub" (p. 152). When he hands the slide back to Wilson, he leaves his own fingerprints on it. Wilson recognizes them as matching the set on the murder weapon, and realizes the long deception, and solves the current mystery. Tom, mistaking Wilson's sudden excitement for illness, says "Don't take it so hard; a body can't win every time; you'll hang somebody

yet," and Wilson's inaudible answer pronounces judgment
on Tom and brings the novel full circle to that long
forgotten "fatal remark" about an unseen dog: "It is
no lie to say that I am sorry I have to begin with you,
miserable dog though you are!" (p. 153). The Governor's decision, which concludes the novel, merely
implements Wilson's early remark and later judgment,
confirming "dog" as the lowest common denominator for
"man." In pardoning Tom so that Percy Driscoll's cred-
itors could sell this heretofore invisible piece of
property down the river, the Governor has effectively
silenced the loudmouth who had in so many ways disturbed the community, severed him from the identity and
status he had so long enjoyed, and upheld the cause of
law and order and a kind of justice.

III

Critics who view Wilson as the hero of the story
tend to ignore two important factors: first, the
inconsistency between the fictional character of
Pudd'nhead Wilson in the story and the hazy, transcen-
dent persona responsible for the "Calendar," and
second, Twain's own description of what he intended
Wilson to be. It would be too much to insist that the
bifurcated character of Pudd'nhead Wilson is thematically appropriate to the novel, but it is even less
justifiable to view Wilson as a largely sympathetic
character reflecting the author's own opinions. Henry
Nash Smith has cited Twain's estimate of Wilson as he
expressed it in a letter to Livy in 1894: "I have
never thought of Pudd'nhead as a _character_, but only as
a piece of machinery--a button or a crank or a lever
with a useful function to perform in a machine, but
with no dignity above that."[3] Wilson may be somewhat
sympathetic because of his years of neglect, but he is
essentially unfeeling and only superficially perceptive. In fact the Wilson who participates in the
action of the story does not seem perceptive enough to
have uttered the original remark about killing his half
of the dog or to understand the moral consequence of
such symbolically charged fractional division.

The maxims of the Calendar reflect an aspect of
Wilson we hardly see in the events of the novel. It is
scarcely possible to imagine that the Wilson who osten-

sibly accepts the F.F.V. code and reprimands Tom for
not confronting Luigi in a duel could have produced the
penetrating combination of disillusioned wit, cynicism,
and iconoclasm in the Calendar. And it is scarcely
possible to imagine that the Mark Twain who scorned
chivalry and dueling in <u>Life on the Mississippi</u>,
<u>Huckleberry Finn</u>, and <u>A Connecticut Yankee</u> could admire
the spurious nobility of these pretentiously named
leading citizens. (In fact such names as Judge York
Leicester Driscoll, Percy Northumberland Driscoll, and
Col. Cecil Burleigh Essex recall some of the cast in
Mark Twain's pseudo-Elizabethan farce <u>1601</u> or his bur-
lesques of Shakespeare.) Wilson wants to be recognized
and accepted as part of this village elite, he is
"deeply gratified" by the invitation to run for mayor
of Dawson's Landing, and he considers this political
opportunity "a step upward" (p. 104). In the final
courtroom scene he serves as protector and supporter of
the town's most cherished values and institutions--
including the system of slavery. For such a man to
commemorate Columbus Day by writing "It was wonderful
to find America, but it would have been more wonderful
to miss it" is inconceivable (p. 166). Even the one
remark about a dog in the Calendar is out of keeping
with the meanings attached to "dog" by Wilson or other
members of the community, for the Calendar maxim slyly
praises virtuous caninity at the expense of brutish
humanity: "If you pick up a starving dog and make him
prosperous, he will not bite you. This is the principal difference between a dog and a man" (p. 122). Mark
Twain has apparently presented us with two rather separate characters in his portrayal of Pudd'nhead Wilson.

As a consequence of this cleavage, he felt the
need to supply some exposition to help the reader join
the disparate parts of Wilson's character:

> For some years Wilson had been privately at work
> on a whimsical almanac, for his amusement--a cal-
> endar with a little dab of ostensible philosophy,
> usually in ironical form, appended to each date,
> and the judge . . . read them to some of the chief
> citizens. But irony was not for those people;
> their mental vision was not focused for it. They
> read those playful trifles in the solidest ear-
> nest, and decided without . . . doubt that Dave
> Wilson was a pudd'nhead (pp. 48-49).

Quite clearly, this passage, the most extensive of the "unifying" passages, describes the more satanic author of the Calendar, not his notably less visionary counterpart who ultimately thrives so comfortably within the ethos of Dawson's Landing.

And it is in the context of the Calendar that Wilson's original "fatal remark" must be interpreted. We can then treat it as an example of far-reaching, bitterly ironic wisdom—an exposure of what seems at best human folly and at worst the ineradicable evil in man's nature. Like the entries in the Calendar, it is an indictment justified not by any plausible or realistic relationship to the events of the novel, but rather by its moral perception of what makes mankind tick in this Middle-American community and of where the greatest danger to the community lies. When Wilson utters these first significant words, he appears disengaged, not focused on what concerns the citizens he has just met; he speaks "much as one who is thinking aloud" (p. 25). His remark seems to proceed more from the trancelike realm of prophecy than from observation of an immediate situation, as evidenced by its effect on his audience:

> The group searched his face with curiosity, with anxiety even, but found no light there, no expression they could read. They fell away from him as from something uncanny, and went into privacy to discuss him (p. 25).

As we know, they wholly misconstrue his meaning. For one thing, they miss his irony and ignore his implication; he _knows_ that to kill one half of the dog is to kill the other half too. And as the author of the Calendar he also knows that the citizens are incapable of grasping the moral truth inherent in this graphic image of vivisection—simply that it applies to all aspects of human life, whether physiological, psychological, or social.

The Wilson of the Calendar who can make this point is much closer to Mark Twain than is the unsuccessful lawyer and ardent hobbyist, and only the Calendar character can conceive such a complex analogy wherein for man or for society the whole organism is the fundamental unit of being, and any arbitrary division or artificial quantification for purposes of convenience, profit, or punishment can only mean death. It is doubly ironic that one of the witnesses to Wilson's remark expresses this basic principle when trying to determine Wilson's hypothetical responsibility as a property owner (of his half of the dog): "if he killed his half and the other half died, he would be responsible for that half just the same as if he had killed that half instead of his own" (p. 25). What this man fails to realize is that this idea lies at the heart of Wilson's lesson in fractions. And the society of Dawson's Landing fails to realize that there is little or no moral distinction between the overt violence that can result in physical death and the covert violence that can result in psychic death.

Wilson's "joke," then, describes the essentially destructive effect of division and disunity on certain key, natural relationships symbolically represented in the ideal of the living organism; and the idea behind the joke is closely tied to the twin motif in <u>Pudd'nhead Wilson</u>. Even <u>Those Extraordinary Twins</u>, the rudimentary farce from which <u>Pudd'nhead</u> was extracted, reinforces this suggestion. The story originally centered on a pair of Siamese twins--"a combination consisting of two heads and four arms joined to a single body and a single pair of legs"--a single organism but exhibiting two distinct personalities, often at odds with one another (p. 170). Twain envisioned various sorts of conflicts between the two "halves" of his twins--fights over deportment, drinking, lovemaking, etc. Of course, certain characteristics of these originals come through in the finished, separated brothers, Luigi and Angelo. Except for the differences in hair color, the two look exactly alike; they travel together and play the piano together. Essentially they exist as one person. As with Wilson's dog, there seems to be no such thing as an experience, relationship, or consequence capable of affecting one half and not the other. When they reveal Luigi's past history and the murder he committed, Angelo asserts: "He did it to save my life, that's what he did it for. So it was a noble act, and not a thing to be hid in the dark." Luigi's explanation reveals even more:

> You overlook one detail; suppose I hadn't saved Angelo's life, what would have become of mine? If I had let the man kill him, wouldn't he have

killed me, too? I saved my own life, you see (p. 85).

Reflected in the concept of brotherhood, and emblematized in the physical fact of twinhood, the ideal of the organism projects itself above the surface of the novel. Luigi knows instinctively that you can't kill half a dog, and his knowledge of this runs deeper than that of the community. (Mark Twain knew this truth instinctively, too. But whether he was <u>consciously</u> formulating such a doctrine of organicism is impossible to determine. It is quite likely that his esemplastic imagination, set in motion by a highly charged key image, tended thereafter to operate almost on its own, often producing linked images and ideas whose significance he may not have been fully aware of.)

Though they are not physical brothers, the other twins in the story--Tom and Chambers--might as well be. They look alike; as characters, their respective fathers scarcely differ at all and might just as well have been one person. The nebulous Essex is just Percy Driscoll duplicated and peeled off to avoid the embarrassing situation of the white master's adultery with his not so black slave, a liaison that would have required Percy Driscoll to vault out of one bed and leap into another in order to father sons born to different mothers on the same day. The fact that there is no apparent physical difference between Tom and Chambers when they are babies allows Roxy, acting out of mother love, to switch them deliberately without detection. Unfortunately, in protecting one twin, she "sells out" the other and so initiates the chain of events that will "dog her cats" inevitably to tragedy. At this point, the theme of disunity and arbitrary division (the clothes seem to make all the difference), becomes connected with the issues of slavery and betrayal. Roxy praises God for the "salvation" of her son: "Oh, thank de good Lord in Heaven, you's saved! Dey ain't no man kin ever sell mammy's po' little honey down de river now!" (p. 36).

Thus the inexorable machinery of the slave society forces Roxy to commit the act that represents the highest form of evil--the betrayal of a close relationship, whether biological or spiritual--in "selling" the real Tom "down the river," figuratively, when she allows him to assume the identity of a slave. Her own son's later actions magnify the betrayal implicit in her own act of radical division and readjustment, and when he is ultimately sold down the river, the system ironically compensates for her tampering and restores the original arrangement. Either way, however, natural relationships have been sundered and an act of perverse violence has been committed in the killing (or denying the actual existence) of a significant fraction of a living entity.

The act of "killing" one half of the dog, and that of "selling down the river," we are reminded, are symbolic equivalents. Roxy conjoined the two images when she found out that her son had betrayed her: "Sell a pusson down de river--down de river! . . . I wouldn't treat a dog so!" The terms are semi-allegorical references to the same species of evil, examples of which saturate the events of the story. Roxy neglects the child in "tow linen" as much for his lack of apparent "class" as the fact of his not being her "real" son. "Tom" abuses "Chambers," whose place he himself would have occupied had Roxy not interfered. Percy mistreats "Chambers," who is actually his own son, unrecognized by his "master" (p. 42). Tom's own nature, which Roxy refers to as "fractious" (p. 41, a word combining elements of "fractional" and "vicious"), thrives on strife and division among others; he cheers up noticeably when the twins argue, or when Pudd'nhead appears foolish in front of others. He does, however, distribute his hatred evenly: "He hated the one twin for kicking him, and the other for being the kicker's brother" (p. 115). But doubtlessly, the most outrageous incidents of inhumanity and betrayal are the twin acts of sale down the river: Tom sells his mother; the courts of "justice" sell Tom.

The novel suggests further that arbitrary division is by its very nature a form of betrayal which destroys certain fundamental relations based on family, community, and a larger sense of humanity. The society, irrationally and arbitrarily (as it turns out), makes damaging distinctions in regard to race:

> To all intents and purposes Roxy was as white as anybody, but the one sixteenth of her which was black outvoted the other fifteen parts and made her a Negro. She was a slave and salable as such. Her child was thirty-one parts white, and he, too,

was a slave, and by a fiction of law and custom a
Negro (p. 29).

The social effect of these distinctions is to cultivate
disunity by elevating to quasi-sacred status this communal code, this elaborate fiction of human fractions.
By law and custom the identity of an individual could
be quantified by fractional division of blood into
categories of white and black. In the scheme of Mark
Twain's novel, this sort of behavior is a submerged,
slow, unconscious moral masochism--a deep, prolonged,
unhealing social fracture. The town punishes itself by
not only maintaining the false and unnatural distinctions of the slave market, but also by its patently
foolish reverence for F.F.V. pretensions, and their
genteel justification of violence. The false Tom, as
Henry Nash Smith points out, is really the end-product
of Dawson's Landing and, by extension, of the entire
region:

> Although Tom Driscoll is evidently the key figure
> in the imaginative logic of Pudd'nhead Wilson, he
> is . . . not so much a character as a complex of
> themes. He incarnates both the tortured paradox
> of uncertain identity and the perversions result-
> ing from generations of the bad training imposed
> by slavery.

The most evident source of Tom's duality, according to
Smith, is in his "divided" background, one half of
which is strictly F.F.V. aristocratic--i.e., the part
supplied by his father--while the "other half of Tom's
heritage is that of Roxy, the slave. The two parts of
it are at war with each other."[4]

The politics of the town sustains the image of an
organism in internal war with itself, the traditional
"diseased body politic," familiar from Shakespeare.
The good fellowship of the Sons of Liberty is shown to
be only illusory; the members fight over trifles before
their meeting is over, and apparently are not averse to
the kind of slanderous, brutal campaigning that the
Judge sanctions in order to get Wilson elected mayor.
The farcical image of the "anti-rummies," in the guise
of volunteer firemen joyfully turning their hoses on
their political opponents graphically illustrates the
notion of the village as an unbalanced social organism
working against its own good health and fated to fall

victim to its own internal antagonisms. We should not be amused by the bitter truth that "citizens of that village . . . of a thoughtful and judicious temperament did not insure against fire; they insured against the fire company" (p. 91).

There can be no doubt that Pudd'nhead Wilson is a pessimistic book. It moves relentlessly to show that none in "the land of the free" is truly free and the few who are "brave" measure their courage by an inhumane standard. No one is without taint, not the pure descendant of the F.F.V., not the ambitious intellectual, and certainly not the black in bondage. For a variety of reasons and in different ways, the book proves that "the skin of every human being contains a slave."[5] Tom has opportunities along the way to recognize firsthand the essential brutality and inhumanity of accepting and living in accordance with arbitrary labels and divisions. But neither reform nor escape is part of his nature; both have been driven out of him by a devastating combination of corrupt training and his own innate, unyielding temperament. Roxy, who alone attempts to stand against circumstance and the continuing heinousness of white domination over her, accepts virtually all of the values and institutions cherished by the slave society in which she finds herself. In the end she fails miserably on all counts, and the novel literally offers no way out, not for the false Tom who gets treated as he was so ready to treat others, nor for the true heir, who, despite the fact that he "found himself rich and free" was doubtlessly doomed to lead a dog's life for he "could not endure the terrors of the white man's parlor, and felt at home and at peace nowhere but in the kitchen" (p. 167). Mark Twain chooses not to tell this further story, but it is quite clear that if he had, it would be the continuing story of a house divided against itself, some of its inhabitants at home in the parlor, others knowing their place in the kitchen.

That F. R. Leavis should have found Pudd'nhead Wilson "a profound study" of an admirable civilization paying homage to art, recognizing excellence in its cultural elite, and exhibiting "the outward signs of an inward grace," is quite incredible.[6] We cannot help feeling some note of condescension here--toward America, toward American literature, and toward Mark Twain as an indigenously American writer. Rather than deny the frequently satirical and occasionally subversive tone of <u>Pudd'nhead Wilson</u>, it might be more accurate to view it as a bitter burlesque of what America was supposed to be and a painful depiction of what it had come to be--one nation, under God, infinitely divisible, with a mockery of justice for all.

1. (New York, 1964), xi. Subsequent references to this edition will appear in parentheses in the text.

2. George M. Spangler, "Pudd'nhead Wilson: A Parable of Property," American Literature, 42 (March 1970), 28-37; James M. Cox, Mark Twain: The Fate of Humor (Princeton: Princeton University Press, 1966), pp. 222-46. Spangler cites previous scholarship which has stressed the centrality of either the racial theme or the theme of environmental determinism in the novel, as well as that which has faulted the novel for alleged lack of coherence and clarity. His own essay has greatly helped in understanding the overlapping social and economic meanings, but it has unfortunately also fostered a thematic division present in the previous criticism. To insist on the primacy of "the idea of property, more particularly the obsession with property as a vitiating and reductive influence on human beings" (p. 29) is to relegate the more emotional and sensational racial theme—involving slavery, miscegenation, and painfully arbitrary problems of identity—to a secondary status where it simply refuses to abide. This racial theme pushes forward in much the same way as Mark Twain, in his account of the genesis of the novel, described the more somber implications forcing their way out of the original farce.

3. Mark Twain: The Development of a Writer (Cambridge, 1962), p. 181.

4. Mark Twain, pp. 176-79. Lawrence J. Friedman, in a comment on this essay, has suggested that Mark Twain's theme of a divided society reflects his awareness of the internal oppositions as the views of Hinton Helper vs. those of George Fitzhugh, the protectionism vs. free trade controversy, denominational warfare on the religious scene, and political disagreements in the case of Whig vs. Democrat or in the case of states as South Carolina vs. Virginia. To deny these divisions and present an image of unity in the face of external threats, deviants and scapegoats were persistently required, for they enabled this divided society to effect a form of negative self-identification. He suggests further that in Mark Twain's novel even temporary scapegoats like Wilson or the Italian twins

allowed the representative society of Dawson's Landing to obscure, for a time at least, the realities of regional crisis.

5.   *Mark Twain's Notebook*, ed. Albert B. Paine (New York, 1935), p. 393.

6.   Introduction to *Pudd'nhead Wilson* (New York, 1955), pp. 13-19.

VI

"DO NOT BRING YOUR DOG": MARK TWAIN ON THE MANNERS OF
MOURNING

Most successful humorists cultivate a love-hate
relationship with their audiences; most great writers
extend this relationship to society at large--exposing
its incongruities, puncturing its pomposities, con-
demning its constraints, especially when these social
conventions and expectations suppress and debase any
genuine individual emotion. Mark Twain was a successful humorist who became a great writer because he
learned how to transform caricature and comic confrontation into social criticism and informed sympathy for
the vulnerable, human individual--black or white, Jew
or Gentile, Chinese or Filipino--the individual who was
relatively helpless against the cupidity, stupidity,
and hypocrisy of organized society.

Quite early in his career Mark Twain recognized
"that in order to know a community, one must observe
the style of its funerals," and we see him returning to
this recognition in book after book.[1] More important
we can trace the development of humorist into humanist
(not that the two are necessarily exclusive) as he uses
the socially sacred institution of the funeral to convey the attitudes, values, and manners of his society.

The key to understanding and appreciating Mark
Twain's achievement (as well as his limitation) lies,
as Henry Nash Smith has demonstrated, in Mark Twain's
perception and fictional projection of a central conflict in values in 19th century American society. This
conflict was not geographical or regional; it was not
West versus East; it permeated American society West,
East, North, and South. In assessing Mark Twain's
development, Smith uses the terms "genteel" and "vernacular." The genteel was the dominant culture. It
encompassed the cherished values of accredited spokesmen and women (who played a major role in inculcating
and reinforcing the genteel tradition). It was proper,
cultivated, reverent, idealistic, and patriotic. It
was projected by our institutions of learning, our
houses of worship, the front halls of government, and
the galleries of the few existing museums. It looked

to Europe for principle and precedent and adopted Victorian attitudes and values in uncritical concentration, extending them to Tempe or Tacoma no less than Manhattan or Mainline Philadelphia.[2]

The emergent vernacular tradition was coarse, spontaneous, irreverent, empirical, pragmatic, and occasionally subversive. Its literary origins lay in the language and outlook of the regional humorists to whom Mark Twain apprenticed himself, but whose work he ultimately transcended. Genteel writers depicted a world as it should be, values that were unchanging, and human behavior that was predictably and didactically appropriate. Mark Twain was in the forefront of those who rejected most of the assumptions of the genteel tradition, but his dilemma lay in his being tied to that tradition almost as strongly as he felt the need to repudiate it. His internalized conflict found its expression in the humor of social confrontation and incongruity, and he raised it to an art.

The genteel tradition looked to Europe for its cultural cues, and Mark Twain records his own peculiar pilgrimage in his first book, The Innocents Abroad. In the valedictory note that concludes that book Mark Twain writes that his anticipated "pleasure trip" to Europe and the Holy Land "was a funeral excursion without a corpse." When young Sam Clemens booked passage on a Brotherly Love Boat called The Quaker City, he was immediately beset by the false piety, the social pretense, and the blatant hypocrisy that typified every subsequent funeral in his work. And despite his characterization of the trip, it did not lack a corpse. What Mark Twain tried to bury was the veneration that gentility attached to Europe and to the past. And what he exposed in the process was his deep distaste for the sentimental stock response and excessive gravity that made up the manners of mourning, even when the death had occurred hundreds or thousands of years ago.

Early in the Adventures of Huckleberry Finn, Huck drops his biblical studies when he discovers "that Moses had been dead a considerable long time." His values permit no further intellectual curiosity or emotional investment: "I don't take no stock in dead people," he says in vernacular understatement. It is the same defense that Mark Twain and his unregenerate remnant, who survive the blistering piety of The Quaker

107

<u>City</u> pilgrims, employ to frustrate and destroy the European guides who have invested their livelihood in promoting the veneration of the past. "Is he dead?" consigns Columbus, Michaelangelo, and Leonardo, as well as venerable church martyrs, to the rubbish heap of the past. It is the practical American's seemingly anti-intellectual defense against the aggressively self-righteous gentility that demands a stereotyped approval without any room for the variations of individual appreciation or reaction. The humor of <u>Innocents Abroad</u> marks a rebellion against the closest approximation of ideological conformity known to late 19th century America.

To the veteran of Western mining camps and San Francisco's Barbary Coast the unquestioned veneration of Europe was an assault on human intelligence and humanitarian sensibilities wrought by those who separated the humanities from humanity and who abetted ignorance by merging morbid art and moribund judgment into an amorphous "Renaissance." Museums, cathedrals, morgues, and monasteries seemed to exude the same funereal atmosphere, though they ranged from architectural magnificence to unparalled human misery.

He feels no word of transition is needed to move from the grandeur of Notre Dame to the horrors of the Paris morgue. Recollections of the St. Bartholomew's Massacre and the Reign of Terror are no less oppressive than the unburied dead in the morgue. The depiction of saints and martyrs, fragments of the true cross, some of the original nails, a part of the crown of thorns, the bloodstained robe worn by the Archbishop of Paris when he was shot by insurgents in 1848, his death mask, the bullet that killed him, and the two vertebrae in which it lodged are far more esteemed than the bloody garments of men, women, and children in the morgue. But the latter evoke greater sentiment in the narrator.

His commingled feelings toward the veneration evoked by art, religion, death, and the past are focused by the spectacle beneath the Capuchin monastery in Rome. Having just visited the catacombs, where he calculated the passages as 900 miles and the graves as 7,000,000, he confronts the unique rites of the Capuchin brethren:

Here was a spectacle for sensitive nerves! Evidently the old masters had been at work in this place. There were six divisions in the apartment, and each division was ornamented with a style of decoration peculiar to itself--and these decorations were in every instance formed of human bones!

"Shapely arches . . . of thigh-bones," "pyramids . . . of grinning skulls," "elaborate frescoes whose curving vines were made of knotted human vertebrae" with "delicate tendrils . . . of sinews and tendons" and "flowers . . . formed of knee-caps and toe-nails," lead him facetiously to attribute the designs to Michaelangelo. The bones of 4,000 "departed monks were required to upholster these six parlors," lovingly collected over many centuries and still identifiable as "Brother Anselmo--dead three hundred years" or Brother Alexander or Brother Carlo or Brother Thomas, who died for love of a young woman and whose finger joints now form the veins of a leaf in a floral design.[3]

It is a macabre comment on the mortality of man and the immortality of art with the strong implication that today's monks will find fulfillment in tomorrow's designs. As Mark Twain and his irreverent comrades look at the unused storehouse of future art, the mummified remains of the more recently departed, they see one whose features have shriveled and petrified into a century-old laugh, and they have to struggle to keep from asking the insidious question "Is he dead?"[4]

The extent of anti-Catholic feeling in 19th century America made such irreverence possible, but the circumstance of the Holy Land sacred to all Christians, complicated Mark Twain's task and forced him to alter his strategy. Repelled by the trappings of the Holy Sepulcher, which he calls "trumpery gewgaws and tawdry ornamentation," and by the corrosive and combative piety of Christian pilgrims, which requires Turkish guards to keep peace among rival Christian sects and which also required removal of the original Stone of Unction, much chipped by status-seeking Pilgrims, Mark Twain cynically mentions a few false claims and spurious proofs and then turns the joke on himself, sublimating his anger and securing his safe retreat.

109

Close by the Holy Sepulcher, he contrives the Tomb of Adam and indulges himself in a flood of mock sentimentality so often evoked by funeral proprieties:

> The tomb of Adam! How touching it was, here in a land of strangers, far away from home, and friends, and all who cared for me, thus to discover the grave of a blood relation. True, a distant one, but still a relation. The unerring instinct of nature thrilled its recognition. The fountain of my filial affection was stirred to its profoundest depths, and I gave way to tumultuous emotion. I leaned against a pillar and burst into tears. . . . Noble old man--he did not live to see me--he did not live to see his child. And I--I--alas, I did not live to see _him_. Weighed down by sorrow and disappointment, he died before I was born--six thousand brief summers before I was born.[5]

But in this conscious counterfeit of Victorian propriety, he curbs his egotism and self-pity with mock stoicism: "But let us try to bear it with fortitude. Let us trust that he is better off where he is. Let us take comfort in the thought that his loss is our eternal gain."

Mark Twain's next book _Roughing It_ draws upon experiences prior to _Innocents Abroad_, experiences en route to Nevada and California mine fields and an emerging career in journalism that took him beyond the West Coast to the Sandwich Islands. He describes four funerals, three of them introducing comic veins which he later mines more deeply for purposes of fiction.

The least consequential of the funerals is an irrelevant anecdote in the string of grotesque irrelevancies that make up Jim Blaine's meandering stream of associations set off by recollections of his grandfather's old ram. This stream never reaches its conclusion, as Blaine's colorful distractions include too many obstacles, such as the funeral of William Wheeler. A surrealistic account of trying to observe sacred social proprieties in an age of rapid social change, the story of Wheeler's demise is enough to frustrate any conscientious undertaker. Wheeler "got nipped by the machinery in a carpet factory and went through in less than a quarter of a minute," and in Jim Blaine's words:

> His widder bought the piece of carpet that had his remains wove in, and people come a hundred miles to 'tend the funeral. There was fourteen yards in that piece. She wouldn't let them roll him up, but planted him just so—full length. The church was middling small where they preached the funeral, and they had to let one end of the coffin stick out of the window. They didn't bury him—they planted one end, and let him stand up, same as a monument.

And to conclude this episode of wall-to-wall piety, "they nailed a sign on it." It bore the legend "Sacred to the memory of fourteen yards of three-ply carpet containing all that was mortal of William Wheeler (Ch. LIII)."

Mark Twain's account of Buck Fanshaw's funeral is less concerned with the funeral than with contrasting Western slang and Eastern cultivated discourse. Resembling vernacular-genteel opposition, the sketch is too extreme in its linguistic hyperbole and too much like a vaudeville skit to be artistically significant, but it also has elements that anticipate the greater artistry of the books to come.

In the confrontation between Scotty Briggs, a rough hewn silver miner and the new minister, fresh from an Eastern theological seminary, Mark Twain settles for stereotypes in character and in language. Neither is accurate and we have the comedy of incongruity without a significant conflict in values. Both Scotty and the minister want the same thing: a pretentious funeral for Buck Fanshaw, the deceased saloon keeper, greatly mourned, Mark Twain tells us condescendingly, "especially in the vast bottom stratum of society." When Scotty uses terms like "passed in his checks," "gone up the flume," and "throwed up the sponge," the minister evinces no understanding. "You don't smoke me and I don't smoke you," expresses Scotty's frustration. Only when he resorts to "kicked the bucket," does one of Scotty's slangy metaphorical euphemisms communicate to the minister, whose elevated euphemistic equivalent "Ah—has departed to that mysterious country from whose bourne no traveler returns" is just too opaque for Scotty.

Scotty wants a "gospel sharp" "to jerk a little chin music and waltz him through handsome." The minister would be pleased to "preach the funeral discourse" and "assist at the obsequies." Even though Scotty has never used the word "obsequies" before, and mispronounces it, it establishes a common link between the effete minister and rough miner. Scotty tells him that since Buck "was always nifty himself, . . . his funeral ain't going to be no slouch--solid siver doorplate on his coffin, six plumes on the hearse, and a nigger on the box in a biled shirt and a plug hat. . . . And we'll take care of you, pard. . . . There'll be a kerridge for you; and whatever you want, you just 'scape and we'll 'tend to it."

There is only the faintest suggestion that funerals are of direct benefit to the living rather than the dead or that Scotty and the minister might reinforce their self-importance on this occasion. But like the word "obsequies," which will be resurrected for future funerals, the germs of these suggestions are present in a paragraph whose details might well have been taken from what Sam Clemens as reporter contributed to the Virginia City Territorial Enterprise:

The obsequies were all that "the boys" could desire. Such a marvel of funeral pomp had never been seen in Virginia. The plumed hearse, the dirge-breathing brass bands, the closed marts of business, the flags drooping at half-mast, the long, plodding procession of uniformed secret societies, military batallions, and fire companies, draped engines, carriages of officials, and citizens in vehicles and on foot, attracted multitudes of spectators to the sidewalks, roofs, and windows; and for years afterward, the degree of grandeur attained by any civic display in Virginia was determined by comparison with Buck Fanshaw's funeral.

Scotty Briggs, as a pallbearer and mourner, occupied a prominent place at the funeral (Ch. XLVII).

Only in the lawless egalitarianism of the Western mining towns could a citizen distinguished mainly by his mediocrity and his belligerance be accorded so royal a treatment. Scotty, the apparent representative of vernacular values, fully accepts the genteel conception of funeral proprieties.

The relationship between Scotty and the minister grew stronger, Scotty became conspicuous by his belated conversion to Christianity, and his effectiveness as a Sunday school teacher was enhanced by his customary language--neither he nor his students being aware "that any violence was being done to the sacred proprieties."

The "sacred proprieties" were not exclusive to European or American society. During the Hawaiian interlude, near the end of Roughing It, Mark Twain describes two more funerals, one of which he witnessed and the other about which he read. Both of these were of island royalty and both bore similarities to Buck Fanshaw's funeral. The first was the funeral of Her Royal Highness the Princess Victoria and the second the funeral of her ancestor Kamehameha the Conqueror. (I suspect that any similarity to British royalty, living or dead, was more than coincidental.)

As an American correspondent reporting on foreign customs to an American audience, Twain can afford to be critical without offending anyone by his violence to sacred proprieties. He cites the royal custom by which "the remains had lain in state at the palace thirty days," the nightly pandemonium . . . [of] howlings and wailings, the "beating of tom-toms, and dancing of the . . . forbidden hula-hula by half-clad maidens to . . . songs of questionable decency." He reprints the entire two-page program, listing participants in their priority and wondering whether anyone will be left to constitute the "Hawaiian Population Generally," as called for in the program. The procession was genuinely impressive, composed of the king and his chiefs, officers of the kingdom, foreign consuls, and ambassadors, etc. Mark Twain is particularly impressed by the deference shown toward the king and by his generally democratic and unpretentious demeanor--in contrast to a Mr. Harris, whom he identifies as "the Yankee prime minister": "This feeble personage had crape enough around his hat to express the grief of an entire nation, and as usual he neglected no opportunity of making himself conspicuous and exciting the admiration of the simple Kanakas." So even at this foreign funeral, the largest ego on display belonged to an American (Ch. LXVIII).

In many ways King Kamahameha's funeral was markedly more barbaric, but in some ways it also resembled that of Princess Victoria or Buck Fanshaw. The conspicuous expenditure at the funeral of this much beloved monarch included the sacrifice of 300 dogs-- a divergence from the custom requiring human victims, but since dogs were raised and fattened for food, their sacrifice was an act of conspicuous and wasteful non-consumption. Mark Twain again uses the word "obsequies" to stand for the sacred proprieties of funeral customs, and without any intended irony also uses the word "orgies" to describe the "saturnalia" that customarily accompanied an important funeral in this primitive society: "The people shaved their heads, knocked out a tooth or two, plucked out an eye sometimes, cut, bruised, mutilated, or burned their flesh, got drunk, burned each other's huts, maimed or murdered one another . . . and both sexes gave themselves up to brutal and unbridled licentiousness." To an American writing in the early 1870's even the eroticism of half-clad hula-hula dancers, and "songs of questionable decency" could justify the word "orgies," but certainly the complex intrigues and rivalries surrounding Kamehameha's death as well as the physical and emotional excesses by which his people expressed their grief evoke so condescending and judgmental a phrase as "frightful orgies." The surprise is that "obsequies" and "orgies" will reappear in a respectable middle-American setting as Mark Twain employs the inspired technique of copying from himself in <u>Adventures of Huckleberry Finn</u>.

But before he completes that masterwork, he describes two other Mississippi River funerals, one doubly fictional and the other oppressively factual. For the townsfolk of Mark Twain's fictional St. Petersburg in <u>The Adventures of Tom Sawyer</u>, the funeral of Tom, Joe Harper, and Huck Finn is painfully real. The boys had been missing for a week, their empty raft was found several miles downstream, they must be dead. Because the reader knows that the boys have been camping on Jackson's Island and that Tom had snuck back and learned of the funeral preparations, the funeral is comic, even absurd. Thus the focus really shifts from the circumstances of the funeral to the behavior of the mourners. Since one of the cloyingly successful conceits of Tom Sawyer is the way children unrealistically parody adult folly, the book amuses readers, most of whom miss any implicit criticism. For example, Becky Thatcher berates herself for recollected cruelty to Tom, longs for something associated with his memory, and laments "I'll never never never see him any more." Mark Twain adds "This thought broke her down and she wandered away, with the tears rolling down her cheeks." What seemed melodramatic pathos is self-indulgent bathos (Ch. 17).

Because we know the boys are alive, we can focus even more clearly on the absurdity of their friends' behavior. Grieving classmates are less concerned with the boys' deaths than with the self-importance they can derive from describing how Tom did this and Joe said that and where I stood and who saw them last: "when it was ultimately decided who did see the departed last, and exchanged the last words with them, the lucky parties took upon themselves a sort of sacred importance."

The adult audience at the funeral overflows the church, not because the boys were so beloved but because the townsfolk love a good show and the prospect of being moved to sympathy; the bereaved families can provide both. The funeral sermon provides a further histrionic opportunity for the clergyman, who enlarges upon "the graces, the winning ways, and the rare promise of the lost lads." The audience, responding properly, forgets the faults, flaws, and rascalities of the boys in life, and is moved to tears by the minister's recalling how generous, noble, and beautiful were these boys' characters: "till at last the whole company broke down and joined the weeping mourners in a chorus of anxious sobs, the preacher himself giving way to his feelings, and crying in the pulpit." The key to what is happening and what Mark Twain thinks of it lies in the words "broke down." Becky, the minister, and the congregation manipulate themselves or let themselves be manipulated into a false show of grief, the stock response that shows how all individuality, rational judgment, and hold on reality have broken down. Mark Twain at Adam's tomb, Scotty Briggs in Virginia City, the royal funerals in Hawaii, and the mourners in Tom Sawyer illustrate obsequy becoming orgy.

When the boys appear, the minister who sees them first, "stood transfixed." At the climactic moment of ego gratification, he drops from the center of attention. But like a true trouper, he reacts by stealing back some of the shifted attention: "Praise God from whom all blessings flow--Sing--and put your hearts in it!" Their voices shook the rafters in a burst of communal unity, and "as the 'sold' congregation trooped out they said they would almost be willing to be made ridiculous again to hear Old Hundred sung like that once more." They had been sequentially "sold"--once by the minister, once by their own hunger for sensation, and once by the boys. But they got more than the emotional catharsis they sought--stirred to sympathy, moved by mourning, and yet nobody had to die. Moreover, Mark Twain has moved his focus on funerals closer to home, unburdened himself a bit, and yet avoided offending anyone.

By the time Mark Twain published <u>Life on the Mississippi</u> in 1883, he took himself quite seriously and expected others to do so, too. He is no longer the reporter, tourist, correspondent, or nostalgic storyteller; he has become the outraged consumer advocate and social activist, contemptuous of hypocrisy and offended by business practices. The funeral industry must have hated Mark Twain as they hated Jessica Mitford for exposing "the American way of death." New Orleans, where the dead are entombed in vaults, rather than buried in the ground, gives him opportunity to sound off forcefully. First he complains that the marble cities of the dead are kept much cleaner and neater than the nearby business districts. He values the fresh flowers but detests the ugly, inexpensive, and virtually indestructible <u>immortelle</u>, "which is a wreath or cross . . . made of rosettes of black linen, with sometimes a yellow rosette at the conjunction of the cross's bars. . . . The <u>immortelle</u> requires no attention: you just hang it up, and there you are; just leave it alone, it will take care of your grief for you, and keep it in mind better than you can; stands weather first rate, and lasts like boiler iron." He admires the graceful little chameleons that scamper across the marble vaults but suggests that their talents have been overrated: "They change color when a person comes along and hangs up an <u>immortelle</u>; but that is nothing: any right-feeling reptile would do that" (Ch. XLIII).

He cites health problems stemming from burial, whether above or below ground, he cites statistics to show that money expended on funerals far exceeds money spent on the public schools in the United States, and he builds the argument for cremation. But most of all the embittered Mark Twain is outraged by the poor being victimized when they are most vulnerable, and he is most offended by the kind of person who thrives on such victims. Recalling the plight of "a colored acquaintance" who is hard-pressed to support a wife and several children on what he makes at odd jobs and manual labor. The death of a child was a financial disaster to him: "he walked all over town . . . trying to find a coffin that was within his means. He bought the cheapest one he could find, plain wood, stained. It cost him twenty-six dollars. It would have cost less than four . . . if it had been built to put something useful into."

He reserves his bitterest economic and moral outrage for the character of an ex-insurance man, now an undertaker. Six or seven years had passed since he last saw this man, but the man is more youthful, cheerful, and prosperous than ever. Unlike the uncertainties of the insurance business, the man proudly announces the consistent superiority of his new trade: "No, sir, they drop off right along--there ain't any dull spots in the undertaker line." His success has enabled him to move from attic quarters to an impressive new house. In answer to Twain's question about the profit in coffins, he answers ingratiatingly: "Look here; there's one thing in this world which isn't ever cheap. That's a coffin. There's one thing in this world which a person don't ever try to jew you down on. That's a coffin. There's one thing in this world which a person don't say, 'I'll look around . . . and if . . . I can't do better I'll come back and take it?' That's a coffin. There's one thing in this world which a person won't take in pine if he can go walnut, and won't take in walnut if he can go mahogany; and won't take in mahogany if he can go an iron casket with silver doorplate and bronze handles. That's a coffin. And there's one thing in this world which you don't have to worry around after a person to get him to pay for. And that's a coffin." Twain is depicting not a "right-feeling reptile," but a reptile, nevertheless, and he lets the man's vocabulary and grammar convey his values.

This man boasts of how the rich must have the best and are willing to pay for it and how if you work a poor man right, "he'll bust himself on a single layout." And especially vulnerable is a poor widow who wants to maintain her pride and self-respect. Embalming charges are just as lucrative: "There ain't anything equal to it but trading rats for di'monds in time of famine." When he also adds that a fashionable funeral, lasting several days, takes lots of ice, and "we charge jewelry rates for that ice," he lays out his primary values. The stench of those values offends Twain more than the thought of Princess Victoria's lying thirty days in iceless state. Although his anger is directed at the unscrupulous, hypocritical, chemeleon-like undertaker, more than a little strikes the surrounding society whose sentimentality, fraudulent aspirations, and excessive concern for funeral proprieties make it so vulnerable to the manipulations of a conniving confidence man.[6]

It is more than a matter of historical and cultural curiosity that the second part of Life on the Mississippi, the part that occasioned Sam Clemens' return to the River in 1882, also enabled him to resume work on Huckleberry Finn. From Chapter 17 on, Mark Twain drew heavily on his largely negative impressions of Mississippi communities which he had so recently revisited. The Grangerford family, with whom Huck stays until he is reunited with Jim, provides a microcosm of American Victorian bad taste and false values. A whole panorama of editorial outrage from Life on the Mississippi comes to life in Huckleberry Finn, whether directed at architecture, interior decor, education, art and music, family feuds, or modes of worship. Even earlier books suggest possibilities that take on new meaning and relevance in Huckleberry Finn. The self-dramatized grief of Becky Thatcher's "I'll never never never see him anymore" becomes Emmeline Grangerford's treacly laments "Shall I Never See Thee More Alas" or, if the deceased happened to have been a bird, "I Shall Never Hear They Sweet Chirrup More Alas," or her more ambitious "Ode to Stephen Dowling Bots, Dec'd." Emmeline's purpose in life was to compose such funereal tributes, and now that Emmeline lies dead and buried Huck tries "to sweat out a verse or two" in her behalf. To his credit he is not up to the task.

Much more adept at fraud and deception are those two grand fakes, the duke and the king. We know them only from their shifting identities and the improbable bombast that constitutes their social credentials. They take on roles far more readily than the chameleon can change its hue, and among their immediate ancestors are such respectable businessmen that make their livelihood on the Mississippi as the sellers of oleomargarine for butter and cottonseed for olive oil, or more directly, that thoroughly unwholesome undertaker who has grown rich on others' misery.

When the duke and the king find an opportunity to fleece a grieving family, they stoop to the occasion. Posing as brothers to the recently dead and as yet unburied Peter Wilks, they pull out all emotional stops and let the tears fall where they may. When a grown man cries copiously and wails "Alas, alas, our poor brother—gone, and we never got to see him: oh, it's too, too hard!" and all this in a fake English accent, Mark Twain at Adam's Tomb or Emmeline Grangerford with crayon and pen seem unduly restrained. These two con men take one look into the coffin,

> then they bust out a crying so you could a heard them to Orleans, most; and then they put their arms around each other's necks, and hung their chins over each other's shoulders; and then for three minutes, or maybe four, I never see two men leak the way they done. And mind you, everybody was doing the same; and the place was that damp I never see anything like it. Then one of them got on one side of the coffin, and t'other on t'other side, and they kneeled down and rested their foreheads on the coffin, and let on to pray all to theirselves. Well, when it come to that, it worked the crowd like you never see anything like it, and so everybody broke down and went to sobbing right out loud. . . .

> Well, by-and-by the king he gets up and comes forward and slobbers out a speech, all full of tears and flapdoodle about its being a sore trial for him and his poor brother to lose the diseased, and to miss seeing diseased alive, after the long journey of four thousand mile, but its a trial that's sweetened and sanctified to us by this dear sympathy and these holy tears, and so he thanks

119

them out of his heart and out of his brother's
heart, because out of their mouths they can't,
words being too weak and cold, and all that kind
of rot and slush, till it was just sickening; and
then he blubbers out a pious goody-goody Amen, and
turns himself loose and goes to crying fit to bust
(Ch. XXV).

Mark Twain has finally found the means of exposing
excessive gentility and hypocritical piety without
exposing himself. Huck has no social status to protect
and no perverse concept of sacred proprieties to
defend. He can see that the deluded and manipulated
mourners have "broke down," but he can add a kind of
fresh derision and covert vernacular metaphor that Mark
Twain could not voice himself. What broke the crowd
down into mindless sentimentality was the calculated
show of grief that "worked the crowd." An even coarser
character than Huck, for example Mark Twain's earlier
caricature of white-trash attitudes, Thomas Jefferson
Snodgrass, could habitually refer to something that
affected him emotionally as having "worked me worse'n
castor oil." This metaphor is part of Huck's world,
and it tells us even more forcefully than words like
"slobbers," "blubbers," "flapdoodle," "soul-butter,"
and "hogwash" what Huck thinks of this controlled
catharsis and the flood of sentimentality it produces.

The king and the duke have more than deception on
their minds; they mean to defraud Peter Wilks' daugh-
ters of their legacy. Having "sold" themselves as
brothers from abroad, they are emboldened to over-reach
themselves in improvised pretense. Reaching back to
Buck Fanshaw's and King Kamehameha's funerals, Mark
Twain finally makes his obsequies-orgies joke work. In
his lavish invitation to all the townspeople to attend
the funeral, the king repeatedly uses the phrase
"funeral orgies" and when the duke slips him a note to
tell him he means "obsequies" not "orgies," the king
confidently explains: "I say orgies, not because it's
the common term--but because orgies is the right term.
Obsequies ain't used in England no more now--it's gone
out. We say orgies now, in England. Orgies is better,
because it means the thing you're after, more exact.
It's a word that's made up out'n the Greek _orgo_, outside, open, abroad; and the Hebrew _jeesum_, to plant,
cover up, hence inter. So, you see, funeral orgies is
an open er public funeral." The town doctor laughs at

this spurious display of learning, but, no one will believe him, and both the deception and the funeral plans proceed.

The false brothers are conspicuous for their sobs and handkerchiefs. The townspeople file past the coffin and look in momentarily, some dropping a tear. The undertaker is a masterful rustic, described in terms alternately cat-like and reptilian:

> he slid around in his black groves with his softy soothering ways, putting on the last touches, . . . and making no more sound than a cat. He never spoke; he moved people around, he squeezed in late ones, he opened up passage-ways, and done it all with nods and signs with his hands. Then he took his place over against the wall. He was the softest, glidingest, stealthiest man I ever see; and there weren't no more smile to him than there is to a ham.

In the midst of the sermon, an outrageous racket comes from the cellar, drowning out the minister and disturbing the solemnities. But the undertaker is up to the emergency. He glides quietly around two sides of the room and down into the cellar, from which they hear a loud whack, "a most amazing howl or two," and then dead silence. The minister resumes, the undertaker returns, gliding slowly, his back and shoulders against the wall, making his way around three sides of the room. Finally the revelation everyone awaits: he "rose up, and shaded his mouth with his hands, and stretched his neck out towards the preacher, over the people's heads, and says, in a kind of coarse whisper, 'He had a rat!' Then he drooped down and glided along the wall again to his place." It is nice to know that the dog's howling was not a reaction to the sermon or the squeaky melodeon, it is nice to know that Huck is civil enough to reflect that "the funeral sermon was very good," and it is equally nice to know that he is honest enough to add "but pison long and tiresome."

Mark Twain's method, which must have involved recalling the details and vocabulary of every funeral he described, might convince some of the existence of an artistic providence which put a chameleon, an undertaker, an earnest minister, a prime minister, and 300 dogs just where he could find them and use them again.

121

Others might conclude that his art had forced him out of the closet and into the admission that pious observance of the sacred proprieties frequently led to orgies of hypocritical sentimentality.

Mark Twain recognized that funerals were among the most revered and the most revealing ceremonies in Victorian America. In a society dedicated to progress and prosperity, social proprieties could be more important than business proprieties. He must have been impressed by both the earnestness and the absurdity of the etiquette books that proliferated in the last half of the 19th century. These books disclose the insecurity of the upwardly mobile and the absolute power of genteel authority. We have seen Emily Post give way to Miss Manners and Ann Landers, but the earnestness and the insecurity are still there, even when the questions are far more candid and intimate. For the sake of both the insecure and the self-assured, Mark Twain also turned his hand toward advice on proper behavior. His unfinished book of etiquette, if followed precisely, would seem to guard against funeral obsequies becoming orgies. It includes a number of prescriptive imperatives, all stated negatively, such as "Do not criticize the person in whose honor the entertainment is given." He warns against criticizing the funeral "equipment," even if the handles are only plated, and against any overt or covert sign of disagreement with the description of the character and history of the principal. The advice is simultaneously cynical and earnest, often assuming that hypocrisy is the norm. At other times it is chillingly proper:

> At the moving passages, be moved—but only according to the degree of your intimacy with the parties giving the entertainment, or with the party in whose honor the entertainment is given. Where a blood relation sobs, an intimate friend should choke up, a distant acquaintance should sigh, a stranger should merely fumble sympathetically with his handkerchief. Where the occasion is military, the emotions should be graded according to military rank, the highest officer present taking precedence in emotional violence, and the rest modifying their feelings according to their position in the service.[7]

Only the military paradigm conveys the full weight of prescribed social behavior and the clearly totalitarian quality of the genteel establishment. Mark Twain's last prohibition for funeral etiquette is covertly a prayer that conveys an opposite meaning, an unvoiced plea, that someone may disobey his final injunction: "Do not bring your dog." And we know why--a dog cannot be trained to observe the sacred proprieties. People, unfortunately, are different.

1. <u>Roughing It</u>, Ch. XLVII.

2. <u>Mark Twain: The Development of a Writer</u> (Cambridge, 1962), Ch. 1.

3. Ch. 28 in one-volume editions; Ch. 1, V. 2, in two-volume editions.

4. The century-old petrified laugh is a slightly more polite version of the century-old petrified man that Mark Twain described in an early contribution to the Virginia City <u>Territorial Enterprise</u>. This humorous hoax also counterpoints the gravity of death and the grossness of life: "The body was in a sitting posture and leaning against a huge mass of croppings; the attitude was pensive, the right thumb resting against the side of the nose; the left thumb partially supported the chin, . . . and the fingers of the right hand spread apart." The hoax depends on the reader noticing the similarity of "croppings" and droppings, the pensive posture of <u>The Thinker</u>, the crude way of venting the left nostril, and the permanence of the nose thumbing sign. After determining that the man died of "protracted exposure," the people tried to bury the body but found that the water dripping down his back had "deposited a limestone sediment" that glued him to his seat. The regional judge ruled against blasting him loose, because "such a course would be little less than sacrilege." Washoe County thus acquired a new and enduring tourist attraction.

5. Ch. 53 in one-volume editions; Ch. 26, V. 2, in two-volume editions.

6. Mark Twain's undertaker has a contemporary ally in a Phoenix Baptist minister who replied to a newspaper reporter's question about funeral expense: "Jesus had a very good burial and not one line of the gospel indicated his tomb was too lavish or expensive. I take a very dim view of people who play down an expensive funeral because it can be a very beautiful thing, helpful for the family. Besides, I have a profound admiration for the body. I can talk about pure spirit all I want, but I am in the body, and it has been a pretty good friend to me. I would like it to be

laid down as gently as possible, and look as much like it did in life as possible." To protect our local economy and raise the gross national product, I do not reveal the name of the minister or the date on which his comments appeared in The Phoenix Gazette.

7. Letters from the Earth, ed. by Bernard DeVoto (New York, 1963), p. 152.

"No More Water, the Fire Next Time":   The Continuity of
American Apocalyptic Thought

I

The course of American apocalyptic writing has
been an intriguing and persistent one in our historical
consciousness.   Its origins lay in the sacred ambigu-
ities and veiled portents of Revelation, but it assumed
important national and international ramifications and
extensions in the revolutionary movements of the 18th,
19th, and 20th centuries.   For most of its history
American apocalyptic thought has been optimistic, positing a struggle between the long suffering forces of
good and the temporarily successful forces of evil.
The sequence was thought to involve several stages:
(1) a period of tribulation for the remnant that had
assumed the role of ancient Israel, (2) the coming of
the charismatic leader who leads the remnant to victory
at Armageddon, (3) a millennial period of improvement
during which Satan is bound for 1,000 years and the
souls of the martyred saints are delivered to Christ,
(4) the loosing of Satan who rallies the forces of evil
for a last effort before being destroyed by "fire from
heaven," and (5) the transformation that produces a
"new heaven and a new earth" and renders final judgment
on all who through the ages had followed the way of
Babylon.

The New Jerusalem stands as the actualized Kingdom
of God or, from the secular perspective, a period of
accomplished   social   reorganization,   economic
transformation, and political reconstruction.   In the
cosmology of apocalypse the terminal destruction is a
redemptive event; the ultimate conflict and catastrophe
are essential to the providential scheme of Christian
deliverance.   Only in recent times have the pessimistic
connotations of "apocalypse" come to dominate, as the
powers of unprecedented destruction are seen to reside
in man's hands more than in God's hands.   Whether the
vehicle of destruction is military technology, the
product of chemistry laboratory, or the result of bio-
genetic engineering, we have seen fact mirror fantasy
in a way that makes science fiction far more real than
its gothic predecessors ever were.

During the past 20 years, scholars and critics have investigated and discussed this subject from a variety of perspectives and with varying purposes.[1] But fortunately for my purposes, their varying perspectives and concerns enable an overview, based on specific examples from the 17th century to the 20th, that draws from their efforts and, while striving for fresh insights, might at least offer some old insights more freshly.

From Puritan pulpits and from the pens of our earliest historians, the unique purpose of American settlement was to hasten the end of the known world and to unveil the New Jerusalem. Even the most fervent Doomsday sermons, like Wigglesworth's incongruous ballad, inspired the faithful (while attempting to terrify and redirect the doubtful) by stressing the prospect of the most divine and supernatural light at the end of the historical tunnel. Edward Johnson, town clerk of Woburn, whose <u>Wonder-Working Providence of Sions Saviour in New England, 1628-1651</u> first appeared in 1653, is in every sense a primary source of information. Because of the delayed publication of Bradford's far better known history, Johnson's <u>Wonder-Working Providence</u> was until the second half of the 19th century the only available first-hand record of the events of early settlement.

In a passage addressing "all yee Nations of the World," some of whose citizens together with the New England remnant shall constitute "the Seed of Israel," Johnson announces that "the ratling of your dead bones is at hand." With strong counselors, judges, and warriors "to fight for you, . . . then sure your deliverance shall be sudden and wonderfull." The resurrection of the dead will dwarf the miracles performed in "your fore-Fathers deliverance" from Pharoah, and it will announce "your deliverance upon the whole World, by Fiers and Bloud destroying both Pope and Turke, when you shall see great smoake and flames ascending up on high, of that great Whore." In Puritan typology Babylon and Rome were one, and they would be obliterated by a wrathful and long-suffering Christ, whose army would be the "People of Israel gather[ed] together as one Man." Standing in battle against the Satanic forces of Gog and Magog, they would release "Rivers of bloud, and up to the Horse-bridles, even the bloud of those [who] have drunke bloud so long." With conspic-

uous joy Johnson rhapsodizes "Oh! dreadful day . . .
What wonderous workes are now suddenly to be wrought
for the accomplishment of these things!" He and his
fellow New Englanders are "the forerunners of Christs
Army, and the marvelous providences . . . [are] the
very Finger of God." If the nations of the world be
skeptical, Johnson tries to overcome their doubt by his
rapid-fire rhetoric of question and answer: "Will you
not believe that a Nation can be borne in a day? here
is a worke come very neare it."[2]

It is embarrassingly clear that Johnson considered
the Papacy and the Ottoman Empire the institutions of
the Antichrist, but to Pope and Turk he would add the
American Indian as the third foot of Satan's tripod.
There is little compassion for the Indian and little
sympathy for those New England folk who included the
Indian in their sense of mission. In any dispute with
the Indians, Johnson was ready to suggest that the
specific incident was part of the long-standing issue
with Satan. If Indians succumbed rapidly to European
maladies to which they had no resistance, Johnson would
view the circumstance as another providential favor to
the more resistant New Englanders. (The Rev. Jerry
Falwell takes the same view of homosexuals and the AIDS
epidemic.) In his book of verse Good News from New-
England, published in London in 1648, Johnson dispar-
aged the Indians as "men that naked been whom labour
did not tame." They were savage because they had no
visible vocation and damned because they made no lasting improvement in a natural environment which they did
not seek to possess (p. 6).

The American mission implemented the biblical
injunction to exercise dominion over and to subdue
nature, and this religious imperative to labor,
exploit, and improve further extended white superiority
over the Indian. Good News from New-England begins
with admiration for "this Western world with store of
mettels clear extraction"; and Book III of Wonder-
Working Providence, charting the route of Henry
Thoreau's two-centuries-later trip on the Concord and
Merrimack Rivers and discussing the settlement of
Salisbury and Haverhill, further describes the domes-
tication and domination of the wilderness:

The constant penetrating farther into this Wilderness hath caused the wild and uncouth woods to be

fil'd with frequented wayes, and the large rivers to be over-laid with Bridges passeable, both for horse and foot (p. 234).

Johnson's language has, as John Seelye has noted in _Prophetic Waters_, a distinctly "linear, technological thrust" (p. 229). Since Thoreau's _Week_ will also command close attention in my survey of American apocalyptic writing, it is of interest to note that in his account of the settlement of Concord, Johnson cites "a faire fresh River," with alewives and shad in season but lacking salmon and dace because of the barrier presented by the rocky falls, which also flood some valuable meadowland. Attempts to cut through the falls have failed, but Johnson suggests that a solution lies "with an hundred pound charge"--perhaps the first instance in American writing to suggest that what God's miraculous providence has not accomplished, man's explosive ingenuity may yet bring about. Even more important is Johnson's readiness to tame the turbulence of the river for purpose of profit and convenience (p. 110).

If Edward Johnson sounds like James G. Watt, our now infamous former Secretary of the Interior, the similarity is far from accidental. Sacvan Bercovitch wrote in his analysis of _The American Jeremiad_ that in the Puritan church-state "theology was wedded to politics and politics to the progress of the kingdom of God," and Watt's Interior policy was calculated to re-assert this theocratic principle (p. xiv). Secretary Watt may have seemed to be following economic rather than religious imperatives, but the American mission long ago yoked these imperatives, and a passage from Johnson's _Wonder-Working Providence_ could apply as easily to oil leases as land holdings. Noting that "there being an over-weaning desire in most men after Medow land, which hath caused many towns to grasp more into their hands then they could afterward possibly hold," he immediately adds that "the people are laborious in the gaining the goods of life, yet are they not unmindful also of the chief end of their coming hither" (pp. 234-5). On Johnson's map and apparently on Watt's as well, a millennial kingdom of goods lay en route to the kingdom of God.

There is considerable irony in my suggesting that Secretary Watt was a historical recidivist with incorrigible apocalyptic tendencies, but some of his less sensational comments about the moral and economic state of American Indians strengthen this philosophical link. Citing a variety of social maladjustments and economic dysfunctions which he asserted were widespread among American Indian communities, he placed the blame directly on the Bureau of Indian Affairs and its record of socialistic policies. To compound the irony, Indian leaders reacted only to the initial assertions, which they viewed as isolated racist slanders, rather than part of a long record of denigration, slightly updated by adding the socialistic B.I.A. to the forces of the Antichrist.

Not every adherent of apocalyptic thought shared the Johnson-Watt view of the Indian. Typical of the more liberal, but no more accurate, view was Samuel Sewall, whose personal account of his search for a wife of attractive mien and means humanized the selections from the Puritans in innumerable American literature classes. Sewall wrote a short treatise in 1697, which he formally entitled <u>Phaenomena quaedam Apocalyptica</u> and more informally subtitled "Some Few Lines towards a Description of the New Heaven as It makes to those who stand upon the New Earth." His thesis is that America will be the site of the apocalyptic struggle, and he firmly believes "that the Captain of our Salvation hath [not] landed his Forces here, to disturb and vex Satan only, but to fight with him in good Earnest, and break his Head" (p. 33). In addition to promoting this vivid version of the fight of the centuries, Sewall is much occupied by thought of the Indians and his preface advances the idea (now part of Mormon doctrine) that the "Aboriginal Natives of America" are "Israelites unawares" (p. i). He hopes that they "may avoid the chains of slaves and be delivered among the Children of God" (p. ii). In his diary he recalls a discussion of whether on Judgment Day Negroes might be resurrected as white. No doubt he would extend the same privilege to converted Indians as well. Naive as such conjecture now seems, Sewall's suggestion of apocalyptic assimilation is a more generous view of that wondrous day when, as Johnson phrased it "you People of Israel gather together as one Man, and grow together as one Tree" (p. 60).

II

Probably no one in 18th century America inquired so fully into apocalyptic thought as Jonathan Edwards. Perry Miller, in an essay entitled "The End of the World" called Edwards "the greatest artist of the apocalypse." The recently published volume of the Yale Works of Jonathan Edwards devoted to his Apocalyptic Writings runs to 500 pages, about half devoted to his private "Notes on the Apocalypse" from manuscript and half to his public or published work, An Humble Attempt To Promote Explicit Agreement and Visible Union of God's People in Extraordinary Prayer For the Revival of Religion and the Advancement of Christ's Kingdom on Earth, pursuant to Scripture-Promises and Prophesies Concerning the Last Time (1747). This volume establishes Edwards as the scholar even more than the artist of the apocalypse. He read widely in science as well as in theology in his effort to validate the apocalypse and establish its time table. But in this effort, as in so much of his life, there lies a tragic nobility in his extensive endeavors to build a contemporary foundation for an idea that was losing its currency. It was Edwards' peculiar fate to stand with providence and predestination as they yielded to natural law, to stress the subordination of man to God as that idea yielded to natural rights, and to maintain a religious conception of the millennium even as it yielded from within itself a growing secular faith in the idea of progress.

Millennial ideas were no less important in the half-century following Edwards' Humble Attempt, but they flowed in new channels. As Cecelia Tichi explains in New World, New Earth, there was an increasing tendency to view the Age of Liberty as the millennium and to identify America as the beacon and haven for the fullest realization and fulfillment of freedom. Whereas 17th century spokesmen had seen the American mission as religious redemption and deliverance, 18th century shapers of ideas and events saw the Americans as peculiarly chosen to demonstrate the virtues of freedom and to extend them to accomplish a global regeneration. Just as the American Revolution launched the millennial New Earth, the expectation was that France, Poland, Germany, and England would mount insurrections and break the crown of depotism forever--the political counterpart of breaking Satan's head or bruising the serpent's skull. There is more than a little irony that in this first game of revolutionary dominos, it was the American Revolution that constituted the initial action from which the ensuing reactions were to follow.

More than anyone else, Tom Paine tried to make the issue of American independence a matter of global importance, going so far as to attempt to influence the direction of the fall of the French domino. In Common Sense, which so quickened the pace of American events after its 1776 publication, he wrote: "We have it in our power to begin the world over again. A situation, similar to the present, hath not happened since the days of Noah until now. The birthday of a new world is at hand." In the history of apocalyptic thought there is an immense gap between Edward Johnson, Samuel Sewall, and Tom Paine: but it seems only a short step from Paine's 18th century exhortation to the unknown author of the 20th century appeal to global insurrection:

> Arise, you pris'ners of starvation!
> Arise, you wretched of the earth.
> For justice thunders condemnation.
> A better world's in birth.
>
> . . . . . .
>
> Arise, you slaves, no more in thrall.
> The earth shall rise on new foundations,
> We have been naught, we shall be all.
>
> 'Tis the final conflict,
> Let each stand in his place,
> The Internationale shall be
> The human race!

The rise of Marxism as a social, political, and economic philosophy has systematized many of the secular aspects of apocalyptic thought, but in the 18th and early 19th centuries the sources of political millennialism were nearly always sacred in character and usually so in expression.

An unlikely ally to Paine in the export of revolutionary principles was Joel Barlow, who, when remembered at all, is linked to the comic verse of "Hasty

Pudding." Following a political trajectory that took him from early religious, political, and poetic conservatism to friendship and political intimacy with Jefferson and diplomatic service under Madison, Barlow published (almost simultaneously with Paine's <u>Rights of Man</u>) a two-part treatise entitled <u>Advice to the Privileged Orders, in the Several States of Europe, Resulting from the Necessity and Propriety of a General Revolution in the Principle of Government</u>. The title amply evinces the purpose of the work; but even before Part II appeared in print, Barlow composed and sent a lengthy <u>Letter Addressed to the People of Piedmont, on the Advantages of the French Revolution and the Necessity of Adopting Its Principles in Italy</u>, which was not published in English until three years later in 1795. It was to Barlow that Paine turned for help when he was arrested by extremist forces in France in late 1793, but Barlow was more successful in his rescue of the manuscript of <u>The Age of Reason</u> than he was in securing freedom for Paine, who spent nearly a year in a French prison. Until his death in Poland in late 1812, an indirect casualty of Napoleon's disastrous dream of conquest, Barlow remained a missionary in service to the idea of America as the herald of the political millennium and the reconstruction of the world.

In some of Barlow's poetry, however, lay other aspects of apocalyptic thought that mark the route to major 19th century concerns. In 1783 Barlow completed work on a long philosophical epic, which he called <u>The Vision of Columbus</u>. In this poem, published in 1787, Barlow used the narrative device of Columbus and a mentor-angel exploring the past, present, and future aspects of America. Drawing upon Milton for narrative strategy and Pope for poetic form, Barlow consciously tried to reflect and to shape American values during those conservative years that produced the Constitution. It was an ambitious but a safe poem, and it only barely hints at the intellectual changes that Barlow would undergo in the next two decades.

These changes, political and psychological, were responses to his increasingly liberal social and political acquaintances and to his broadening experiences in France and England. They prompted him to follow the advice that Henry Thoreau would write in the "Conclusion" of <u>Walden</u>, some 50 years later: "Be a Columbus to whole new continents and worlds within you, opening new channels, not of trade, but of thought." The result was an even more ambitious and apocalyptic epic which Barlow entitled The Columbiad.

Published in 1807, this much-revised version of Columbus' epic tour presents a guardian spirit of the New World named Hesper, who in answer to Columbus' numerous questions reveals the realities, possibilities, and probabilities of American circumstances. Much of their exploration follows American rivers and waterways, and their route includes successive mention of the Delaware, Hudson, Hartford, Charles, Piscateway, Kenebec, [St.] Lawrence, Niagara, the Great Lakes, Mississippi, [St.] Peter, [St.] Croix, Ohio, Yazoo, Black, Illinois, Moine, Francis, Rouge, Missouri, Chesapeak, Wabash, Monongahela, Roanoke, Albemarle, Pamlico, Santee, Savanna, Oconee, Monmouth, Connecticut, and Narraganset. By comparison, Thoreau's Week on the Concord and Merrimack Rivers, another utterly serious work with marked apocalyptic overtones, would seem a very minor, mock-epic and a much lesser atlas of rivers real, literary, and legendary.

Much more than the earlier Vision, The Columbiad celebrates not only American accomplishment but also continuing progress in science, agriculture, technology, and the fine arts. All of these are included in Columbus' observation that "Far in the Midland, safe from every foe, / Thy arts shall flourish as thy virtues grow." In its emphasis on scientific investigation and practical application as evidence that American life had reached a millennial stage, there is the strong supposition that the ultimate defeat of error and ignorance would mark the New Jerusalem. The Columbiad is a pragmatic poem--a series of proposals for a NSF, NEH, NIH, FEPC, and SSRC conceived long before anyone put the alphabet to such use. The result would be a world of peace, health, comfort, convenience, and utility. A common language would obviate all misunderstanding, and, no less remarkable, North and South America would join in enduring political union.

In this millennial vision of America all discovery and learning is to be shared, and what is immediately good for America is ultimately good for the world:

> The mind shall soar; the coming age expand
> Their arts and lore to every barbarous land;
> And buried gold, drawn copious from the mine,
> Give wings to commerce and the world refine.
>
> Mold a fair model for the realms of earth,
> Call moral nature to a second birth,
> Reach, renovate the world's great social plan
> And here commence the sober sense of man.

Although Barlow would have us believe that we have reached the millennium and that the New Jerusalem was not far behind, he did introduce an element of serious uncertainty. Adherence to liberty and civic virtue must be more fully understood and its principles expanded to eliminate the anomaly of slavery. Its continuation was more than a political paradox in paradise, and Atlas, Africa's guardian spirit, delivers an Enlightenment Jeremiad, threatening cataclysmic upheaval of this New Earth if old wrongs are not rectified. America thus faces a choice between deliverance and destruction--precisely the message of James Baldwin's The Fire Next Time (1963). But Barlow believes in cosmic affirmative action and the enlightened avoidance of catastrophe.

In Book X, the final segment in Columbus' guided tour of the New Earth in the New World, Barlow offers a prevision of a world in peace blessed with the mutuality of one language and with the material and moral progress stemming from the expanded role of science and ethics:

> Till mutual love commands all strife to cease,
> And earth join joyous in the songs of peace.
> Thus heard Columbus, eager to behold
> The famed Apocalypse its years unfold;

The first part of the apocalyptic preview would occasion no outcry, but the second clearly gives an Enlightenment view of the Antichrist. Although when Barlow was questioned about his "disrespect" for the cross, he answered by referring to his early religious antipathy to Catholicism and his identification of the cross with Rome. Barlow had come a long way from any reference to breaking Satan's or the Pope's head, but he had not forgotten from where he started:

Let heaven unfolding show the eternal throne,
And all the concave flame in one clear sun;
On clouds of fire, with angels at his side,
The Prince of Peace, the King of Salem ride,
With smiles of love to greet the bridal earth,
Call slumbering ages to a second birth,
With all his white-robed millions fill the train,
And here commence the interminable reign!

Beneath the footstool all destructive things,
The mask of priesthood and the mace of kings,
Lie trampled in the dust; for here at last
Fraud, folly, error all their emblems cast.
Each envoy here unloads his wearied hand
Of some old idol from his native land;
One flings a pagod on the mingled heap,
One lays a crescent, one a cross to sleep;
Swords, sceptres, mitres, crowns and globes and
stars,
Codes of false fame and stimulants to wars
Sink in the settling mass; since guild began,
These are the agents of the woes of man.

The final part of this preview of apocalypse integrates
Revelation and the Newtonian world view in a mode that
is more progressive than that of Sir Isaac Newton--who
was himself a serious student of apocalyptic lore and
prediction:

> Till one confederate, condependent sway
> Spread with the sun and bound the walks of day,
> One centred system, one all ruling soul
> Live thro the parts and regulate the whole.

Among the works that Barlow left unfinished was a
manuscript entitled "The Canal: A Poem on the Application of Physical Science to Political Economy."
Begun as a joint effort with Robert Fulton, who was to
be Barlow's technical consultant, the 290 line fragment
is less than one-fourth of the projected four books.
Like _The Columbiad_, it dates from the end of the 18th
and beginning of the 19th centuries; but even more than
The Columbiad, it makes clear that science and technology constitute the mainstays of the millennium and the
agents of apocalyptic deliverance.[3]

Appropriately enough, there is no mention of beauty in nature, only of delight in profiting from its exploitation, utilization, and refinement:

Yes, my dear Fulton, let use seize the lyre,
And give to Science all the Muse's fire,
Mount on the boat, and as it glides along,
We'll cheer the long Canal with useful song.

The task of Fulton, whose plans at this time included not only the steamship but a submarine, would be

To teach from theory, from practice show
The Powers of State, that 'tis no harm to know;
And prove how Science with these Powers combined,
May raise, improve, and harmonize mankind.

There is no sense of the picturesque but an unlikely union of the sacred and the secular sublime in Barlow's praise for the force which "Curbs with strong dikes" the river's "boundless waste of wave, / And wakes whole countries from their watry grave." Waste in nature is a sin that technology must redeem; and by "waste" Barlow means rivers without mills or barges, fields without farmers, and mineral deposits without mines. Frances Trollope, gazing at the unspoiled beauty of a wilderness river scene in upstate New York about 1830, fortunately captured this sentiment in the words of a Yankee passenger who was more speculator than spectator: "If you was to see it five years hence, you would not know it again; I'll engage there will be by that, half a score elegant factories--'tis a true shame to let such a privilege of water lie idle."4

Barlow's millennial America would not lack saviors or fiendish opponents. Fulton, a failed artist, would fulfill his messianic destiny in the annals of invention and industry. In Barlow's prophecy he would be joined by "some future Franklin" who will "trace the germs of meteors thro the realms of space" and force the airborne coupling of hydrogen and oxygen, thereby ending the rule of both "Demon Drought" and "the Fiend of Fever." Our scientific savior will employ this man-made rain to baptise the New Earth and make the deserts bear flower, fruit, and trees. There is a further appropriateness in linking the spirit of Franklin to this messiah of the mechanic arts because

Philadelphia had suffered a plague in 1793, and Barlow describes the Fiend that spreads the plague thusly:

> On clouds of fire she mounts the loaded air,
> And shakes contagion from her slimy hair,
> O'er Philadelphia spires her station gains,
> Broods o'er the stifled streets and crowded fanes,
> Hot from her putrid pores, as forth they crawl,
> Worm after worm, the ripe diseases fall. . . .
> O'er the dumb town one funeral crape is spread,
> And one wide grave ingulphs a thousand dead.

Surprisingly, Barlow's imagination of apocalypse is as vivid as that of a Mather or an Edwards, but the characters in the drama have shifted. In this Enlightenment Armageddon the ingenious rainmaker ends the grip of drought and disease--the new Antichrist:

> Ah! seize the Demon, he seals the skies,
> Sink the foul Fiend, no more on Earth to rise.

For the revisionist apocalypse, mankind must manipulate nature and demonstrate mastery through progressive utilization of environmental resources. Only at the stage of maximum mastery can the full possibility of the New Jerusalem be realized and mankind delivered from the crushing physical forces in untamed nature and the corrupting social forces of past political systems.

One longs to fault Barlow for lacking any concern for the environmental impact of his policies and proposals, but it would be foolish to do so. He may not be the only poet-technocrat in American literature, but he is certainly the only one for whom such a thoroughgoing confidence in technology and optimism about the future was possible.

III

A surprisingly thorough and occasionally trenchant response to Barlow's Apocalyptic optimism lies (too little known or recognized) in Henry Thoreau's A Week on the Concord and Merrimack Rivers. In the course of that book, Thoreau manages to indicate his knowledge of Edward Johnson and Jonathan Edwards as well.

Thoreau's _Week_ is more ambitious but less artistically successful than _Walden_, which pessimistically surveys the moral and spiritual condition of American society but optimistically holds forth the prospect of individual regeneration for correctly intuiting the epiphanic symbolism of "Spring." The explicit message of _Walden_ is that "a better world's in birth" but it is a New Earth obtainable only by the route of highly charged and keenly honed metaphor. Literally and figuratively, the imagination is the only means of transport in _Walden_. In the _Week_, we have at least the conveyance of a small boat, two sets of oars, two masts (one of which doubled as tent-pole), and several long poles for shoving through the shallows. But it is still the imagination that charts and navigates the depths.

The _Week_ is the book that Thoreau wrote during his two-year stay at Walden and is thus very close to a climactic point in his life and to the even more climactic composition of _Walden_ that followed. It is an exploration and a celebration of the role of the river in the world's history and in New England's psycho-history. The river is a stream of continental consciousness. Metaphorically, it constitutes a route or channel for an excessively literary and remarkably portentous inquiry into individual and societal values-against a backdrop of no longer unspoiled American nature and the no longer present American Indian. Both have already receded into historical recollection, which Thoreau is consciously refashioning into cultural myth.

Barlow was a pragmatist in his view of America's rivers, lakes, and canals; Thoreau an absolutist and an idealist. His distance from Barlow is well indicated by the subversive double meanings of words he chose to italicize in this passage describing the Merrimack, taken from the "Sunday" chapter:

> Unfitted to some extent for the purposes of commerce by the sand-bar at its mouth, see how this river was devoted from the first to the service of manufactures. Issuing from the iron region of Franconia, and flowing through still uncut forests, by inexhaustible ledges of granite, with Squam, and Winnepisiogee, and Newfound, and Massabesic lakes for its millponds, it falls over

a succession of natural dams, where it has been offering its _privileges_ in vain for ages, until at last the Yankee race came to _improve_ them. Standing here at its mouth, look up its sparkling stream to its source,--a silver cascade which falls all the way from the White Mountains to the sea,--and behold a city on each successive plateau, a busy colony of human beaver around every fall. Not to mention Newburyport and Haverhill, see Lawrence, and Lowell, and Nashua, and Manchester, and Concord, gleaming one above the other. When at length it has escaped from under the last of the factories it has a level and unmolested passage to the sea, a mere _waste water_, as it were, bearing little with it but its fame; its pleasant course revealed by the morning fog which hangs over it, and the sails of the few small vessels which transact the commerce of Haverhill and Newburyport. But its real vessels are railroad cars, and its true and main stream, flowing by an iron channel further south, may be traced by a long line of vapor amid the hills, which no morning wind ever disperses, to where it empties into the sea at Boston. This side is the louder murmur now. Instead of the scream of a fish-hawk scaring the fishes, is heard the whistle of the steam-engine arousing a country to its progress.[5]

The undercurrent of Thoreau's prose is physiological, suggesting sexual exploitation and scatological consequences. The paragraph--beginning with its syntactically and significantly obstructive reference to "the sand-bar at [the river's] mouth," its being "devoted . . . to the service of manufactures," its "offering its _privileges_," its escape "from under the last of the factories" to "a level and unmolested passage to the sea," and its release as industrial _excreta_, "a mere _waste water_, as it were"--could have been written as answer to Barlow's pragmatic hyperbole or Trollope's practical Yankee. Thoreau makes them both seem panderers for industry. In Thoreau's iconology the instruments and advocates of industrial progress are even more clearly agents of the contra-millennium.

If Barlow thought the canal so sublime an example of a pragmatic Providence unfolding an era of millennial progress, Thoreau perceives a more sinister design, as, also in the "Sunday" chapter, he describes his brother and himself leaving the natural channel of the Concord and entering the canal that leads to the Merrimack:

> But now . . . we heard this staid and primitive river rushing to her fall. . . . We here left its channel, just above the Billerica Falls, and entered the canal, which runs, or rather is conducted, six miles through the woods to the Merrimack at Middlesex.

Suggesting the offensiveness of this improper captivity, he indicates their haste to put it behind them: "As we did not care to loiter in this part of our voyage, . . . we accomplished the whole distance in little more than an hour." At a decent distance from this distasteful scene, he reflects that "this canal, which is the oldest in the country, and has even an antique look beside the more modern railroads, is fed by the Concord, so that we were still floating on its familiar waters." But some, he goes on to suggest, have presumed too greatly upon this familiarity, for the canal represents "so much water which the river _lets_ for the advantage of commerce" (p. 62). Again italicizing the idiom of the day which could apply as easily to sexual exploitation as to the utilization of natural resources, Thoreau subtly implies the imaginative links between a falling river, a fallen woman, and the imminent fall of mankind in a previously unfallen New World. Brilliantly and perceptively perverse, Thoreau finds what the majority praises as beneficial progress to be his perdition.

In a largely favorable review, James Russell Lowell chided Thoreau for inviting us on a river-party and holding us in mid-stream while he preached an almost endless sermon. To an Edward Johnson, a Cotton Mather, or a Jonathan Edwards, to whom an exceedingly lengthy sermon would hardly appear sinful, Thoreau would appear far more culpable, an exceedingly dangerous blasphemer. He consciously chooses to use his "Sunday" chapter to launch an attack on the religious establishment more vitriolic than was Emerson's "Divinity School Address." (Thoreau establishes an etymological, i.e. a literal and a figurative link between "re_lig_ion" and "_lig_ature," so that contemporary, conventional worship would appear to be putting the mind into the stocks [p. 64]). But Thoreau's most grievous heresy was his inversion of the conventional alignment in the apocalyptic struggle, so that the forces of good and evil identified by his 17th and 18th century forbears actually switched roles in the Week. As he himself recognized in Walden: "The greater part of what my neighbors call good I believe in my soul to be bad, and if I repent of anything, it is very likely to be my good behavior. What demon possessed me that I behaved so well." In his reversal of this traditional moral alignment, Thoreau strengthened the negative implications of apocalyptic thought and initiated the tendencies that became more prominent in the work of Melville (especially his short fiction and The Confidence-Man), Emily Dickinson, Mark Twain, and Henry Adams in the 19th century and T. S. Eliot, Faulkner, Nathanael West, Flannery O'Connor, Robert Lowell, Ellison, Baldwin, Wright, Barth, Heller, Vonnegut, and Pynchon, to name some of the more conspicuous examples in the 20th century.

Thoreau's strategy in compressing two weeks' travel in 1839 and a decade's work into A Week on the Concord and Merrimack Rivers can be best discerned by viewing his philosophical, historical, and literary efforts in the format of a drama. The cast of characters includes Henry and his brother John (fused into a single narrative consciousness), the current New Englanders they occasionally meet and the many whose names are in record and legend but whose acts and values have shaped the present, and the vanishing or vanished Indian, whose character and claims are still controversial. The set would have to include a small boat, a farm, an Indian village, and several apple trees. Most important of all is the changing and changed wilderness into which the brothers' errand takes them. The Week is for Thoreau a very holy week, and while their destination might be the White Mountains, their quest is for deliverance.

The Indian is the unseen major protagonist even in the introductory section, although Thoreau with dramatic concealment goes no further than a reference to "an extinct race." He has, however, prefixed these lines, the first of many quotations from Emerson:

> Beneath low hills, in the broad interval
> Through which at will our Indian rivulet
> Winds mindful still of sannup and of squaw,

142

Whose pipe and arrow oft the plough unburies,
Here, in pine houses, built of new-fallen trees,
Supplanters of the tribe, the farmers dwell.

"Sannup and squaw" (husband and wife), "pipe and arrow," plough and pine houses, "supplanters of the tribe," farmers and new fallen trees: these are characters in our drama of domestic relationships, peace and violence, settlement and social change. Thoreau opens his book by giving the Indian name for the Concord River, "The Musketaquid," defining it as "Grass-ground River," suggesting that it is "as old as the Nile or Euphrates," and associating the meaning of its name with the phrase "as long as grass grows and water runs." Thus the Indian name for the Concord echoes the phrase used as a vernacular Indian designation for eternity. Yet less than three-quarters of a century after the American call for independence, the Indian is already "an extinct race" (p. 5).

After ironic references to the creativity and moderation of the Concord residents (with no time to write, they clear, burn, scratch, harrow, and plow the earth), Thoreau quotes in full the passage from "old Johnson . . . in his 'Wonder-working Providence'" that suggests altering and improving the river channel with a 100 pound charge of dynamite. But to Thoreau, the Concord is no less noble than "many a famous river on the other side of the globe"--the Xanthus, Helicon, Mississippi, Ganges, and Nile; and he intends his less than epic exploration to reveal the distorted values of his epoch (pp. 9-11).

The vanished Indians had been pitted against the forces of civilized improvement: the builders of the dam and canal at Billerica and the factories at Lowell and the farmers who plant the fields and orchards of Old England in the New World. First they destroyed the fish, and then the Indians whose economy required the fish. Like Edward Abbey's Monkey-Wrench Gang, Thoreau longs to try "a crowbar against that Billerica dam" (p. 37). But even such a grand gesture could not bring back the Indian or divert the process which so completely destroyed a culture and a race.

Central to this process is the simple, celebrated, independent yeoman. Creating an archetypal white farmer to contrast with his archetypal Indian, Thoreau writes in "Sunday":

> Some spring the white man came, built him a house, and made a clearing here, letting in the sun, dried up a farm, piled up the old gray stones in fences, cut down the pines . . . , planted orchard seeds brought from the old country, and persuaded the civil apple tree to blossom next to the wild pine and the juniper. . . . He culled the graceful elm from out the woods and from the riverside, and so refined and smoothed his village plot (p. 52).

The "village plot" calls for the extension of agriculture in the very process that eliminates all traces of agriculture, i.e., all traces of the wild. Even the act of planting becomes in Thoreau's lexicon of values an obscenity:

> He rudely bridged the stream, and drove his team afield into the river meadows, cut the wild grass, and laid bare the homes of beaver, otter, muskrat, and with the whetting of his scythe scared off the deer and bear. He set up a mill, and fields of English grain sprang in the virgin soil. And with his grain he scattered the seeds of the dandelion and the wild trefoil over the meadows, mingling his English flowers with the wild native ones. The bristling burdock, the sweet scented catnip, and the humble yarrow, planted themselves along his woodland road. . . . And thus he plants a town. The white man's mullein soon reigned in Indian corn-fields, and sweet scented English grasses clothed the new soil. Where, then could the Red Man set his foot? The honey bee hummed through the Massachusetts woods, and sipped the wild flowers round the Indian's wigwam, perchance unnoticed when, with prophetic warning, it stung the Red child's hand, forerunner of that industrious tribe that was to come and pluck the wild flower of his race up by the root (pp. 52-3).

The "village plot" thickens considerably as the transplanted European plants civilization: "He buys the Indian's moccasins and baskets, then buys his hunting grounds, and at length forgets where he is buried, and plows up his bones." In the process many Indian

144

place names are discarded and new ones planted: "He comes with a list of ancient Saxon, Norman, and Celtic names, and strews them up and down this river." Thoreau takes his stand against the era "in which men cultivate the apple, and the amenities of the garden" and longs to "strike my spade into the earth with such careless freedom but accuracy as the woodpecker his bill into a tree. . . . What have I to do with plows? I cut another furrow than you see" (pp. 53-4).

Thoreau was, of course, no sexual profligate, but he apparently enjoyed the word play that attached sexual innuendo to the actions of respectable farmers and villagers and sanctioned the freedom of Indian life:

> We talk of civilizing the Indian, but that is not the name for his improvement. By the wary independence and aloofness of his dim forest life he preserves his intercourse with his native gods, and is admitted from time to time to a rare and peculiar society with nature. He has glances of starry recognition to which our saloons are strangers. The steady illumination of his genius . . . is like the faint but satisfying light of the stars compared with the dazzling but ineffectual and short lived blaze of candles (p. 55).

The word "intercourse" provides Thoreau with both overt and covert meanings and the opportunity to cast the American yeoman into an adulterous relationship with nature: "The Indian's intercourse with Nature is at least such as admits of the greatest independence of each. If he is somewhat of a stranger in her midst, the gardener is too much of a familiar. There is something vulgar and foul in the latter's closeness to his mistress, something noble and cleanly in the former's distance" (p. 56). With the molestation of the river and the violation of the land as his broadest charges, Thoreau asserts that civilization itself is the force of evil. In his lexicon to "plant" could be a four-letter word, and "civil" conveys as much enmity and revulsion as "devilish" did for Edward Johnson. Thus the civil English (or by now American) gardener is the satanic agent in the Indians' New World garden.

"Monday" produces another confrontation. Approaching Dunstable, Thoreau recalls that in 1725

Captain Lovewell and his company set out from here in search of "rebel Indians," whom they found and engaged in battle. According to an old ballad, they killed twice their own number of Indians, but lost more than half their company in the fight.

> Our worthy Capt. Lovewell among them there did die,
> They killed Lieut. Robbins, and wounded good young
> Frye,
> Who was our English Chaplin; he many Indians slew,
> And some of them he scalped while bullets round him
> flew (p. 120).

Thoreau, after commenting on the clergyman's trophies of valor, asks (not without irony): "What if the Indians are exterminated, are not savages as grim prowling about the clearings today?" Like Pogo, whose dictum seems to have outlived the comic strip, Thoreau seems to have met the enemy and found that they are us.

"Wednesday" and "Thursday" include two more of the Indian-white confrontations that have such iconographical significance for Thoreau. The first--between Alexander Henry, a fur trader, and Wawatam, an Indian warrior--is in Thoreau's excerpt devoid of the violence that pervades the historical and the literary accounts. At Wawatam's invitation, Henry spends "a long winter of undisturbed and happy intercourse in the family of the chieftain in the wilderness." In his own account of his experiences, Henry wrote "I did not quit the lodge without the most grateful sense of the many acts of goodness . . . nor without the sincerest respect for the virtues I had witnessed among its members" (p. 225).

Despite an earlier reference to cannibalism (Henry's _Travels and Adventures_ goes into great detail about the cannibalism he witnessed, though explaining that it was more a ritual than an atrocity among many tribes), Thoreau writes glowingly of the Wawatam-Henry relationship and says of their idealized friendship: "it has not much human blood in it, but consists with a certain disregard for men and their erections, the Christian duties and humanities, while it purifies the air like electricity. . . . We may call it an essentially heathenish intercourse, free and irresponsible in its nature, and practising all the virtues gratuitously" (pp. 275-6). He means that there is no hint of

146

profit or gain or concern with what one can afford or with one's religious duties. Such Christian concerns turn friendship into charity, heathenish spontaneity into crabbed self-righteousness.

Thoreau's rhetorical purpose in this tale of cross-cultural male bonding is to contrast it with the more sensational cultural encounter of the "Thursday" chapter--the captivity narrative of Hannah Dustan. Like many of the tales of Indian captivity, that of Hannah Dustan was immediate fuel for sermons didactically designed to remind listeners of their religious duties, so that they, like the endangered soul in the narrative, might strive for deliverance. Cotton Mather preached a series of such sermons, based on Mrs. Dustan's harrowing experiences, and one of them, Humiliations Follow'd with Deliverances, was published in 1697. Thoreau's assertion that Mrs. Dustan's capture occurred 142 years before his 1839 trip suggests that Mather's published sermon or something based on it was one of Thoreau's sources. (Mather's sermon was also a source for one of Hawthorne's early expository sketches.)

The captivity narrative was an apocalypse in miniature, a typology of incident, compressing the community's view of its own mythic role and New World experience. The subtitle of Mather's 1697 book makes abundantly clear what a reader should gain from the sermon: A Brief Discourse on the Matter and Method, of that HUMILIATION which would be an hopeful Symptom of our Deliverance from Calamity, Accompanied and Accommodated with a NARRATIVE of a Notable Deliverance lately Received by some English Captives From the Hands of the Cruel Indians and some Improvement of that Narrative. An unsought purpose of such sensational sermonizing, especially when, as in the case of Hannah Dustan, the captives are women, is titillation. For, as Thoreau had written, such events occur in the realm of "men and their erections"--and of their destructions, as he clearly meant to suggest.

Mather's sermon was like a drive-in double feature, as it were, the first starring Hannah Dustan and her nurse Mary Neff and the second featuring Hannah Swarton, both accounts linked by the common theme of "captivity and deliverance" and the thesis "that when a Sinful People Humble themselves before the Almighty

God, it is an Hopeful and an Happy Symptom, that He will not utterly Destroy such a People" (p. 6). His introductory section is a series of more than 20 exhortations, each beginning "Let us humbly confess . . ." and ending with an instance of sinful behavior that could justify God's casting the sinner into circumstances as harrowing as those described in the ensuing narratives. His premise was that public humility now would forestall later private humiliations of the sort borne by the exemplary Hannahs, whose survival ought to instruct their compatriots.

This is not the kind of sermon that would appeal to or influence Henry Thoreau, but it is the kind that would draw his response--in the form of an anti-sermon. In this case, the Hannah Dustan episode is the climactic action of the _Week_ and its meaning is the book's covert denouement. Thoreau begins with details that Mather in his "Improvement" did not include: two lightly clad white women and a boy paddling nervously and unskillfully "down this part of the river," ten still fresh Indian scalps in the bottom of their canoe (p. 320). Thoreau's emphasis is on the retribution Hannah Dustan exacted from her erstwhile captors; Mather's on the degradation and humiliation she endured. In some details, especially the immersion of whites in Indian family life, the narrative resembles Alexander Henry's account, but the total quality cancels the hopefulness of Henry's experience.

Both Mather and Thoreau agree that Hannah Dustan had been forced to leave childbed and in flimsy dress in severe weather had been driven to her captors' wigwam, where accompanied by her nurse, she joined an Indian family of two men, three women, seven children, and an English boy, also a prisoner. Mather cites a difficult march of 150 miles, with inadequate food and lodging; Thoreau says they were taken to "an island in the Merrimack, more than twenty miles above where we now are" (p. 321). Both agree that she had seen seven of her children flee with their father but knew not whether they were alive or dead. She had also seen her infant seized by the ankles and dashed against a tree, but Thoreau supplies the detail of its being an apple tree, an iconographically important detail for him. Both record a further threat: Thoreau, that she and her nurse were to be taken to a distant settlement and forced "to run the gauntlet naked"; Mather, that "they

148

must be Strip't & Scourged, and Run the Gantlet, through the whole Army of Indians" (p. 45). Hannah organizes an escape plan, and the two women and English boy kill all the Indians, save one squaw who managed to escape with one boy. Mather delights in and italicizes his pun that while their captors were in "a Dead Sleep," the English captives, using the Indians' own hatchets, killed 10 of the Indians. But Mather also tells us that they spared the boy (who managed to escape) because they wanted to take him captive. After destroying all but one of the Indians' canoes, they start for Haverhill but after a short distance return for the scalps of the dead to verify their tale. They miraculously reached home safely, "with their trophies," Thoreau tells us, "for which the General Court paid them fifty pounds." And the family of Hannah Dustan was reunited, "except the infant whose brains were dashed out against the apple-tree" (p. 323). Early in his voyage Thoreau had remarked on the farmer's "civil apple-tree"; the final sentence of the final chapter ends the voyage by tying up again to "the wild apple-tree," whose trunk still bore the mark their chain had worn in the previous spring (p. 393). These two trees are the icons of the white man's value system—a system of religion and productivity and the red man's value system—a system of freedom and accommodation to nature. Now he can tell us what this means, but he will only imply, not explicate. First he comments that "there have been many who in later years have lived to say that they had eaten of the fruit of that apple-tree." Then he adds: "This seems a long time ago, and yet it happened since Milton wrote his Paradise Lost," and finally compressing the history of mankind from the Creation and the Fall to the present moment, he indicates how little separates us from the first Fall, how fully immersed we are in enlarging and extending its consequences, and how imminent is the final Apocalyptic act:

The age of the world is great enough for our imaginations, even according to the Mosaic account, without borrowing any years from the geologist. From Adam and Eve at one leap sheer down to the deluge and then through the ancient monarchies, through Babylon and Thebes, Brahma and Abraham, to Greece and the Argonauts; whence we might start again with Orpheus and the Trojan war, the Pyramids and the Olympic games, and Homer and

149

Athens, . . . and after a breathing space at the building of Rome, continue our journey down through Odin and Christ to _____ America. It is a wearisome while. --And yet the lives of but sixty old women, such as live under the hill, say of a century each, strung together, are sufficient to reach over the whole ground. Taking hold of hands they would span the interval from Eve to my own mother. A respectable tea-party merely, --whose gossip would be Universal History. The fourth old woman from myself suckled Columbus, --the ninth was nurse to the Norman Conqueror, --the nineteenth was the Virgin Mary, --the twenty-fourth the Cumaean Sybil, --the thirtieth was at the Trojan war and Helen her name, --the thirty-eighth was Queen Semiramis, --the sixtieth was Eve, the mother of mankind. So much for the --'old woman that lives under the hill, And if she's not gone she lives there still.' It will not take a very great grand-daughter of hers to be in at the death of Time (pp. 324-5).

The passage has many resemblances to earlier attempts, such as those of Jonathan Edwards, to unlock Apocalyptic symbolism by connecting specific historical incidents to the opening of the seals or the breaking of the vials in Revelation, but Thoreau demands a reader as aware of the frivolity as he is of the social seriousness of these pseudo-hermeneutics. The biggest difference in Thoreau's apocalyptic is that he has tried to switch his reader's moral alliances so as to emphasize the negative character of contemporary tendencies: to assert, as it were, that as his Christian cohorts gain in power and influence, things are really getting worse. By his standards, the English settlers were shown a New Earth, which they proceeded to violate, corrupt, and pollute. And in so doing, they performed the devilish work of justifying the extermination of a primitive race by conceiving the realm of the wild and the free as an imagined realm of the fiendish and the fearful. Ultimately they turned the Indian into the satanic abstraction of their religious paranoia. In his perception of the negative implications of American apocalyptic thought, Thoreau is much closer to the temper of the late 20th century than he could ever imagine.

IV

More than a century later, another river trip in a region far removed from Thoreau's Concord repeats the exploration and charts the mental topography of the Week for a new generation of readers--or non-readers, since James Dickey's Deliverance became such a successful motion picture and reached an audience of hundreds of millions in theaters and living rooms, most of whom had no notion of the origin of the title. Also Dickey, whose plaudits as a poet are well deserved, had the good sense, unlike Thoreau, to avoid overloading his prose with his own poetic productions or those of other poets whose works he admired. In Deliverance, first published in 1970 and reprinted several times in the Dell paperback edition I used, we have a novel about four suburbanites whose errand into the wilderness of north Georgia is initially a quest for macho self-fulfillment, but turns into a captivity more humiliating and degrading than Hannah Dustan's, followed by a test of character as harrowing as any imagined by Mather in his account of Dustan's ordeal, and culminating in an ambiguous "deliverance," marked by both survival and tragic loss. Like the Musketaquid and the Merrimack, the North Georgia river of Dickey's Deliverance bears a name that links it to its Indian past. Remote and turbulent, the Cahulawassee will soon be dammed, backing up to inundate virgin forest, rural settlements, and burial places known and unknown. In ways that would have delighted Edward Johnson and Joel Barlow, its hydroelectric power will raise the standard of living, and the new shoreline and water sports will enable the developers to "make it over into one of their heavens," with accessible marinas and motels atop once inaccessible mountains (p. 7). The vast technological effort to subdue, improve, and exploit this wilderness river might be said to stem from Johnson's suggestion of how the Concord River and its surroundings could be improved by the judicious placement of a hundred pound charge. The energy of that charge factored by nearly infinite exponentiality fulfills Thoreau's fears about the apple trees planted by the civilizing New England farmers. But for the multitudes who share the fruit of those trees, it would seem to be a new and better world of man's own making.

In the last autumn before the river ceases to exist as a vigorous, flowing stream, four city men in

two canoes fulfill their leader's fantasy of a weekend's trip down fifty miles of wilderness water. Lewis
Medlock is a physically impressive, inner-directed
auto-didact. The weekend trip is the latest of physical challenges that provide Lewis a Hemingwayesque
source of ethical satisfaction. He is a man of deter-
mination and drive, to the point of obsession, and we
are told that "Lewis wanted to be immortal . . . to
hold on to his body and mind and improve them, to rise
above time" (p. 12). He anticipates a fight for survival when "the machines are going to fail, the political systems are going to fail, and a few men are going
to take to the hills and start over" (p. 40). He is
determined to be one of the fittest.

His closest friend and follower is Ed Gentry, the
narrator. A self-made success as a commercial photog-
rapher with a thriving business, he is nearing forty
and beginning to feel bound by routine and responsibility. He characterizes himself as "a mechanic of the
graphic arts" (p. 28) and "a get-through-the-day man"
with no great aspirations or pretensions (p. 39). Yet
he has not given up "the promise of . . . other things,
another life, deliverance" (p. 30). More tolerant than
Lewis, Ed is also more accepting of their two companions: the somewhat awkward, but normally good-natured
extrovert, Bobby, and the devoted family man and
upright citizen, Drew. Although he makes no claim as
an artist, Ed's eye for detail and design and Drew's
considerable competence as a folk guitarist add human-
istic depth to what might appear superficially a long
story out of _Field and Stream_ or a tale for adult Boy
Scouts.

This is no longer the wilderness of the red man
but "the red-neck South" of maimed farmers and moun-
taineers and of "Jesus Saves" signs. It is also the
land of patent medicines and religious formulas, and
the barnside ads for "666 and Black Draught" draw from
Revelation to purge the evil so that Jesus could save
(p. 37). It is also in Thoreau's phrase the realm of
"men and their erections" and of impending technological change that will transform the topography and
society of the region. In the second day of their
river trip, in what must be one of the most brutal
depictions of the usually comic confrontations of city
slicker and rural hick, Ed and Bobby are held at gun
and knife point. Bobby is sodomized and Ed is about to

be forced into fellatio when Lewis' aluminum hunting arrow silently passes through the chest of the man holding the shotgun on the kneeling Ed. The mountaineer who was about to abuse Ed quickly escapes into the wilderness, and, while the captivity and humiliation are quickly over, the pursuit by vengeance seeking survivor is about to begin. The river's hazards are in no sense diminished by the threat of a depraved pursuer.

Dickey plots his ironies carefully. Though the Indians are gone from this wilderness, the captivity is what Cotton Mather would have glossed as a typological lesson. If Hannah Dustan replicated the tale of Jael and Sisera, Lewis' bow and arrow could be analogous to David's sling. But the fact that it was an arrow is an even stronger historical reminder of the American Indian. The irony is enhanced by the reversal of the stock situation where a simple primitive is to be victimized by a calculating urbanite. Homosexual rape is the last thing one would expect in a pastoral or a wilderness setting, no matter how commonplace it has become in the urban concentration of a prison setting. Although it is unlikely that Dickey's weekend owes anything directly to Thoreau's _Week_, it serves to illustrate what Thoreau drew from the tale of Hannah Dustan: "There have been many who in later years have lived to say that they had eaten of the fruit of that apple-tree," or his earlier warning that even after the extermination of the Indians, there would be "savages as grim prowling about the clearings today." Despite the passage of time and the regional differences, Dickey's _Deliverance_ is as much an apocalypse in miniature and a mythic exploration of American experience as was the formal crafting of the captivity narrative in 17th century New England.

The death of the man who assaulted Bobby creates a further moral dilemma. Drew righteously insists on transporting the body to Aintry, the goal of their trip; Lewis pragmatically summarizes what would happen if they went on trial for murder in a region even more than normally antagonistic to outsiders because of their resentment of the soon-to-be-completed dam. Realizing that their chances of survival would be lessened by the additional burden of the corpse and that their future could be complicated at best or destroyed at worst if they had to deal with local law, they bury

and completely conceal the body and the gun, trusting
that its present remoteness and the waters of the lake-
to-be will hide the grave forever.

Just as they reach the most dangerous stretch of
the river, Drew is shot, both canoes capsize, and Lewis
suffers a broken leg in the churning waters of the
gorge. Worst of all, an unseen assassin waits to pick
them off in the next day's light. Their only chance
lies in outwitting him, making the pursuer unexpectedly
the pursued. And so by moonlight, Ed climbs the cliff
at their backs, hoping that the sniper has not yet had
time to make his way from the point at which he shot
Drew. The dangers of the climb are even greater than
the dangers of the rapids, but Ed reaches the summit
and positions himself in a tree from which he hopes to
put an arrow through the man who he also hopes will
choose this spot to aim at Lewis and Bobby far below.
Battling his own hysteria, Ed shoots an arrow which
critically wounds the man, who nevertheless manages to
shoot at the tree and knock Ed from his perch. In the
fall, he is impaled on his own remaining arrow, which
he has to cut painfully out of his side. After track-
ing the mortally wounded man, lowering his body to the
rocks, and weighting it to sink in the river, Ed can
resume the river trip in the remaining canoe with Bobby
and Lewis. Unlike Hannah Dustan and her companions,
they could only hope that no evidence will link them to
the disappearance of the two captors they had slain.
For that reason they also have to sink Drew's body when
they find it wedged in rocks downstream. A forensic
medicine specialist might well determine that the
crease in his skull had resulted from a rifle bullet.

Out of the wilderness, Ed's wound and Lewis' fracture are both treated in the local hospital. To the
young doctor who is ministering to his wound in the
side, Ed says, "We're lucky we've got you," and the
doctor replies "you're fucking aye, . . . Hands of an
angel" (p. 202). The profane and the sacred remind us
again of the apocalyptic nature of their experience,
and the iconography of Ed's lacerated hands and arrow
in the side is almost excessive in limning the character who has brought two companions back to life.

On the second day of the trip, after the captivity
and the first death, they had to transport the body up
a little stream that flows into the river. They had

to force their way under leaves and branches, which seemed "like a tunnel where nothing human had ever been expected to come," or it seemed "like a long green hall where the water changed tones and temperatures and was much quieter," or it seemed like an "endless water-floored cave of leaves." They stopped "by a sump of some kind, a blue-black seepage of rotten water," around which the earth "was soft and squelchy" and "covered with ferns and leaves that were mulchy like shit" (pp. 114-7). The spot is the locus of physical death and decay, and only after finishing the book does a reader fully realize that this river, like Thoreau's more placid New England rivers, has been a stream of historical consciousness. It is a route to the past such that the weekend excursion recapitulates not only some of the central experience of American settlement but also of the elemental human condition that forces acknowledgment of one's own vulnerability and compels individual participation, even immersion, in the fallen state of man.

For Dickey's characters reflecting on the experience produces no sense of justice or equity. In the narrator's judgment Drew was the best of the group, yet the only one the river claimed. And when Lake Cahula comes into being, not even the river survives--except in the minds of those like Ed and Lewis, whose lives it had so deeply touched. Initially, they hoped that the experience might reinforce their manhood; in the end it has deepened their humanity. If, at the start, Ed could characterize himself as "a mechanic of the graphic arts," he has, by the end of the ordeal, been resurrected to become an artist--a man whose imaginative constructs or creative fictions have to manipulate reality, literally to lie in order to reveal the truth. His coming home effectively fulfills the possibilities of a new life even in the familiarities of his former circumstances.

It was a different set of circumstances that inspired Edward Johnson to write in his <u>Wonder-Working Providence</u>:

As the Lord surrounded his chosen Israel with dangers deepe to make his miraculous deliverance famous throughout, and to the end of the World, so here behold the Lord Christ, having egged a small handfull of his people forth in a forlorne Wildernesse, stripping them naked from all human helps, plunging them in a gulph of miseries, that they may swim for their lives through the Ocean of his Mercies, and land themselves safe in the armes of his compassion (p. 151).

It matters not whether James Dickey had ever heard of Edward Johnson; nor does it matter that Henry Thoreau had read his words carefully. It is only a historical curiosity that John Adams wrote to Jefferson of the odd find that his son, John Quincy, had purchased at a Berlin book auction and sent back home--Johnson's Wonder-Working Providence. What is important is that Johnson's words strike such a continuing, though not constant, chord in American thought and expression. The apocalyptic strain has permeated more than 360 years of American experience, affecting every literary genre and influencing our spiritual and political lives. And it is by no means limited to high culture or to low. In the realm of popular culture it is one of the thoughts common to fundamentalist oratory and to Hollywood films. Although that is another essay which, I am quite certain, is already being written, I find the film phenomenon instructive.

Specifically the cinematic response to the apocalyptic possibilities of thermonuclear destruction or related disaster can be dated from The Day the Earth Stood Still (1951). Nearly four decades of living with the consciousness of The Bomb has produced The Day the Earth Caught Fire (1962) and Dr. Strangelove or: How I Learned to Stop Worrying and Love the Bomb (1964), probably the premier black comedy in this genre. In the late 60's Planet of the Apes (1968) laid the basis for four additional ventures into evolutionary apocalyptic. The 70's began with Gas-s-s-s . . . Or It May Become Necessary to Destroy the World in Order to Save It (1970) and The Omega Man (1971), in which a violence-prone military scientist becomes the unlikely messiah whose sacrifice saves a human remnant from the fanatically religious mutants who worship a nuclear bomb in a post-Armageddon world. The decade culminated in the murky political and literary musings of Apocalypse Now (1979), but an earlier film, the deceptively titled A Boy and His Dog (1975), provided a link to the post-holocaust nightmares of the 80's such as Mad Max (1980) and The Road Warrior (1981). These last two Australian films were remarkably attuned to American experiences and American audiences. More recently Carl Sagan and Paul Ehrlich took a heavily scientific presentation of thermonuclear consequences to Congress, and the ABC presentation of The Day After surprised critics and politicians by attracting one of the largest television audiences of the past decade to this new jeremiad. Subsequently an even larger audience heard the President of the United States admit his interest in Biblical prophesies of the apocalypse and thoughtful viewers might well wonder how future foreign policy might reflect Hollywood endings or evangelical rapture. Unfortunately the discussion did not go far enough for us to determine the extent of his belief that script or scripture promised our redemption by raining "fire from heaven" on the evil empire. But there is historical precedent for believing that America's righteous purpose was to hasten the end of the known world.

In general the cinematic response has been reassuringly negative and pessimistic. I say "reassuringly" because I recently listened to the now late futurist Herman Kahn and he was disturbingly optimistic. If Jonathan Edwards was the 18th century "artist of the apocalypse," Herman Kahn has been its 20th century publicist and evangelist. Decrying the earnest jeremiads of Jonathan Schell's The Fate of the Earth and Robert Jay Lifton's and Richard Falk's Indefensible Weapons and offering his own reassuring titles On Thermonuclear War, Thinking About the Unthinkable, and The Coming Boom (on economic recovery and growth) as reliable alternatives, Kahn urged his audience not to worry about the nuclear threat or about the kind of accommodation that Lifton and Falk call "nuclearism." They argue that the nuclearist comes to view the ultimate destructive force as a divine power, its "fire from heaven" constituting a providential inevitability. Kahn pragmatized this theology of nuclearism and argued that even if the U.S. and the U.S.S.R. were to destroy each other in a thermonuclear confrontation and render the larger part of their territory uninhabitable, it would be only a temporary setback to civilization. By his estimate, a country like India has the know-how and the resources to attain our present level of technological society within a quarter-century, and it was my distinct impression that Kahn of Hudson held forth the hope of Deliverance with a vision of New Delhi as luminous as John of Patmos had of the New Jerusalem.

157

ENDNOTES

1. Among the most useful discussions of apocalyptic influence are R. W. B. Lewis' admirable essay entitled "Days of Wrath and Laughter" in his book <u>Trials of the Word</u> (1965), Ernest L. Tuveson's <u>Redeemer Nation: The Idea of America's Millennial Role</u> (1968), John R. May's <u>Toward a New Earth: Apocalypse in the American Novel</u> (1972), David Ketterer's <u>New Worlds for Old: The Apocalyptic Imagination, Science Fiction, and American Literature</u> (1974), Cecelia Tichi's <u>New World, New Earth: Environmental Reform in American Literature from the Puritans through Whitman</u> (1979), Lakshmi Mani's <u>The Apocalyptic Vision in Nineteenth Century American Fiction</u> (1981), and W. Warren Wagar's <u>Terminal Visions: The Literature of Last Things</u> (1982).

2. All the subsequent references to <u>Johnson's Wonder-Working Providence, 1928-1651</u> are to the edition of J. Franklin Jameson (1910, reprinted 1952). All quotations in this paragraph are from pp. 60-61.

3. Text of "The Canal" is given in K. R. Ball, "Joel Barlow's 'Canal' and Natural Religion," <u>18th Century Studies</u> (Spring 1969), 225-39.

4. <u>Domestic Manners of the Americans</u>, ed. by Donald Smalley (1949), pp. 372-3.

5. <u>A Week on the Concord and Merrimack Rivers</u>, ed. Carl F. Hovde, <u>et al</u>. (1980) pp. 86-7.